GOOD DISAGREEME

GOOD DISAGREEMENT?
GRACE AND TRUTH IN A DIVIDED CHURCH

EDITED BY

ANDREW ATHERSTONE
AND ANDREW GODDARD

LION

Published by Lion Books
an imprint of
Lion Hudson plc
Wilkinson House, Jordan Hill Road,
Oxford OX2 8DR, England
www.lionhudson.com/lion

ISBN 978 0 7459 6835 3
e-ISBN 978 0 7459 6836 0

First edition 2015

Acknowledgments
Every effort has been made to trace and contact copyright owners for material
used in this book. We apologize for any inadvertent omissions or errors.

Extract p. 5 taken from *But I Say to You…* by John Stott, copyright © 1970 John
Stott. Used by permission of Inter-Varsity Press.

Scripture quotations marked NIV are from The Holy Bible, New International
Version, copyright © 1973, 1978, 1984 International Bible Society. Used by
permission of Hodder & Stoughton, a member of the Hodder Headline
Group. All rights reserved. 'NIV' is a trademark of International Bible Society.
UK trademark number 1448790.

Scripture quotations marked ESV are from The Holy Bible, English Standard
Version® (ESV®) copyright © 2001 by Crossway, a publishing ministry of
Good News Publishers. All rights reserved.

Scripture quotations marked NRSV are from The New Revised Standard
Version of the Bible copyright © 1989 by the Division of Christian Education
of the National Council of Churc hes in the USA. Used by permission. All
rights reserved.

A catalogue record for this book is available from the British Library

Printed and bound in the UK, September 2015, LH26

For our church families at St Leonard's, Eynsham, and
St James the Less, Pimlico

Contents

Contributors

Andrew Atherstone is tutor in history and Latimer research fellow at Wycliffe Hall, Oxford, and author of *Archbishop Justin Welby: Risk-taker and Reconciler* (DLT, 2014).

Tory Baucum is rector of Truro Anglican Church in Fairfax, Virginia, chairman of Fresh Expressions USA, and a "six preacher" at Canterbury Cathedral.

Martin Davie is academic consultant to the Church of England Evangelical Council and to the Oxford Centre for Religion and Public Life. He is the author of *Our Inheritance of Faith: A Commentary on the Thirty Nine Articles* (Gilead, 2013) and *Studies on the Bible and Same Sex Relationships since 2003* (Gilead, 2015).

Andrew Goddard is senior research fellow at the Kirby Laing Institute for Christian Ethics (KLICE), Cambridge, and author of *Rowan Williams: His Legacy* (Lion, 2013).

Lis Goddard is vicar of St James the Less, Pimlico, and co-author of *The Gender Agenda: Discovering God's Plan for Church Leadership* (IVP, 2010).

Clare Hendry is assistant minister at Grace Church, Muswell Hill, London, and co-author of *The Gender Agenda: Discovering God's Plan for Church Leadership* (IVP, 2010).

Toby Howarth is Bishop of Bradford, and former secretary for inter-religious affairs to the Archbishop of Canterbury and former national inter-religious affairs adviser for the Church of England.

Ashley Null is research fellow at Humboldt University of Berlin, visiting fellow of the Faculty of Divinity, University of Cambridge, and author of *Thomas Cranmer's Doctrine of Repentance: Renewing the Power to Love* (OUP, 2000).

Ian Paul is honorary assistant professor at the University of Nottingham and managing editor of Grove Books. He is co-author of *Exploring the New Testament* (SPCK, 2011) and co-editor of *We Proclaim the Word of Life* (IVP, 2013), and is a leading blogger on theology at www.psephizo.com.

Stephen Ruttle is a Queen's Counsel, commercial mediator, and arbitrator, and has mediated numerous commercial, business, and government disputes. He is a member of the Church of England's mediation and facilitation team, co-author of the Waging Peace training course, and helps to run a community mediation charity.

Michael B. Thompson is vice-principal of Ridley Hall, Cambridge, and author of *Clothed with Christ* (Wipf and Stock, 2011), *The New Perspective on Paul* (Grove Books, 2002), and *When Should We Divide? Schism and Discipline in the New Testament* (Grove Books, 2004).

Tom Wright is research professor of New Testament and Early Christianity at the University of St Andrews, and former Bishop of Durham. He is author of dozens of books, including *Paul and the Faithfulness of God* (SPCK, 2013), *Paul and His Recent Interpreters* (SPCK, 2015), and the popular *New Testament for Everyone* commentaries.

Foreword

There is not a little irony in the fact that one of the greatest sources of tension between Christians is the issue of how they should disagree with one another. As alluded to at various points in this book, I have spoken of my hope that the Church might model "good disagreement" in living out its differences and conflicts. Yet the telling question mark in this book's title, *Good Disagreement?*, points to the unease which the concept evokes in many people. As the editors set out eloquently in their opening chapter, this unease is often rooted in questions of profound theological importance which it is valuable and essential to explore: can disagreement be "good"? How can we find the balance between grace and truth or (as explored in Tom Wright's excellent fourth chapter) unity and holiness?

This book reminds us that these questions are nothing new. From the first years of the early Church, Christians have grappled with the reality of deep division and have sought to respond in ways which build, rather than hamper, the Kingdom of God. It is very appropriate that Ian Paul's study of the meaning of reconciliation in Pauline theology should be one of the first chapters, laying as it does this crucial foundation: that we seek reconciliation because we have first been reconciled to God in Christ.

It becomes increasingly apparent as we journey through these essays that no "one-size-fits-all" definition of "good disagreement" will suffice. One of the great strengths of this collection is its diversity. Each author writes insightfully from their own experience and expertise, from Reformation history to interfaith dialogue and women's ministry. This allows the full complexity of our calling as reconcilers to shine through, highlighting the subtle, prayerful discernments which each different context demands.

At the same time, there are some common themes which unite many of these accounts of what it means to follow Christ faithfully in a divided Church. I was struck again and again by the importance of truly encountering, in their full humanity, those with whom we disagree. Whether each side has much or little in common with one another, whether the outcome is unanimity or separation, it seems the only way to imitate Christ in our conflicts is to invest trust, love, and time in the people from whom we are currently divided.

What the authors of this book repeatedly and often movingly illustrate is that it is possible – and it is our calling – to uphold both grace and truth, unity and holiness: Christians can engage with one another and their profound differences in an attitude of sacrificial love and openness to Christ. And when they do, the Holy Spirit moves, fellowship is restored and Christian witness is transformed.

Justin Welby, Archbishop of Canterbury

September 2015

1
Disagreeing with Grace

Andrew Atherstone and Andrew Goddard

The history of the church is marred by violent and vociferous disagreements between professing Christians. Even the apostles use language which shocks modern readers, though they also teach grace and gentleness in the midst of conflict. What does it mean to disagree with grace? Shall we simply "agree to disagree"? What about the essentials of the Christian message? This introductory chapter sets the scene for the rest of the book, exploring the language of "good disagreement". It appeals for greater theological clarity, for the significance of individual disputes to be carefully distinguished, and for the church to demonstrate grace in all things.

Insult me again!

One of the most entertaining and also sometimes disturbing theology websites on the Internet is the Lutheran Insulter.[1] It randomly selects an insult from the writings of the great Protestant reformer Martin Luther and then gives you the chance to request "Insult me again". All of the insults are fully referenced from Luther's Works. Some are simply childish ("Snot-nose!"), even if presenting amusing similes ("You are like mouse-dropping in the pepper"). Some are highly personal: writing on marriage Luther exclaims, "Go, you whore, go to the devil for all I care." At times he calls down God's wrath on those with whom he disagrees, especially in his writings against the Roman papacy where he is at his most vehement with challenges such as "May God punish you, I say, you shameless, barefaced liar, devil's mouthpiece, who dares to spit out, before God, before all the angels, before the dear sun, before all the world, your devil's filth." Little wonder the site's designer admits, "I, a Lutheran myself, neither approve of nor condone Luther's insults as appropriate for modern theological discourse, nor most modern discourse for that matter. Some of his insults are inexcusable; a few are so crass as to make me reluctant to put them on this site."

These examples starkly remind us that throughout the history of God's people there have been many instances of "bad disagreement", sometimes involving Christian leaders who nevertheless remain widely respected. Abusive language is only the tip of the iceberg. At their worst – not least during the Reformation – theological disagreements between professing Christians have led beyond violent speech and personal insults to physical intimidation, exile, and imprisonment, even to brutal torture and execution. Five Archbishops of Canterbury have died violently, lynched by the mob, burned at the stake, or beheaded by the axe-man, which has prompted the current archbishop, Justin Welby, to reflect that, mercifully, the worst he has to face is "execution by the daily newspapers".[2] Some divisions between Christians are extremely ancient, propped up by a lengthy list of historic grievances. Competing groups of Orthodox monks (Greek, Armenian, Coptic, Ethiopian, and Syriac) share jurisdiction of the Church of the Holy Sepulchre in Jerusalem, and the brawls and fist fights between them over apparently petty squabbles have become a regular source of amusement for the world's media, but reveal the deeper pain of broken relationships and disagreements handled badly.

The violence of disagreements within the church today – as seen everywhere on the blogosphere – is part of a centuries-old narrative. Professing Christians seem to have an endless capacity for caustic commentary, character assassination, mutual suspicion, and the gushing forth of vitriol, which are signs of a distressing spiritual malaise. As Jesus himself says, "out of the abundance of the heart the mouth speaks" (Matthew 12:34). These internecine hostilities are a public scandal and damage the witness of the church. Christians preach a gospel of grace, but in their own relationships too often demonstrate graceless factionalism. As a result, a watching world grows disillusioned.

Is it possible to transform disagreements within the church from "bad" to "good"? What would it look like for Christians to disagree with grace and to turn cursing into blessing? Can we model relationships which the world finds attractive and countercultural? These are not inward-looking questions for the Christian family, but have massive missional implications.

Christ the controversialist: full of grace and truth

Before you rush to judge the shocking language of theologians like Martin Luther, pause to consider the polemic of the New Testament itself. The apostles never condone physical violence or coercion; rather they call upon believers to suffer with patience for the sake of the gospel, like their Saviour who when reviled did not revile in return (1 Peter 2:23). But when rebuking error they do use extremely strong language, which startles modern readers.

The apostle Paul chastised new converts in Galatia for "deserting the one who called you to live in the grace of Christ" and "turning to a different gospel which is really no gospel at all". He accused some of "trying to pervert the gospel of Christ" and placed them – along with anyone who copied them – "under God's curse" (literally, *anathema*). Later he expressed his wish that such people would go beyond advocating circumcision and "emasculate themselves" (Galatians 1:6–9; 5:12). And this is not just a one-off aberration from the apostle. He warned believers in Philippi to watch out for "those dogs, those evildoers, those mutilators of the flesh", describing them as "enemies of the cross of Christ" whose "destiny is destruction, their god is their stomach, and their glory is in their shame. Their mind is set on earthly things" (Philippians 3:2, 18; NIV).

Indeed, the New Testament never uses soft words for those who lead God's people away from the gospel. Its language would often fail our contemporary tests for "good disagreement":

- "May your money perish with you... You have no part or share in this ministry, because your heart is not right before God" (Acts 8:20; NIV).

- "These people blaspheme in matters they do not understand. They are like unreasoning animals, creatures of instinct, born only to be caught and destroyed, and like animals they too will perish" (2 Peter 2:12; NIV).

- "Certain individuals whose condemnation was written about long ago have secretly slipped in among you. They are ungodly people, who pervert the grace of our God into a license for immorality and deny Jesus Christ our only Sovereign and Lord" (Jude 4; NIV).

- "Any such person is the deceiver and the antichrist" (2 John 1:7).

- "a synagogue of Satan" (Revelation 2:9).

John the Baptist assaults the religious leaders as "You brood of vipers" (Matthew 3:7 and Luke 3:7). But most surprisingly, Jesus himself uses identical language: "You brood of vipers, how can you who are evil say anything good?", "You snakes! You brood of vipers! How will you escape being condemned to hell?" (Matthew 12:34; 23:33; NIV). He pronounces woes on his opponents whom he describes as "blind guides", "blind fools" (*moroi* in Greek, from which we get the word "moron"), and "whitewashed tombs" (Matthew 23:16–17, 27). In John's Gospel, Jesus confronts those who oppose and reject him with the words, "You belong to your father, the devil, and you want to carry out your father's desires" (John 8:44; NIV). Such strong language can even be directed at his closest followers, as in his rebuke to Peter: "Get behind me, Satan!" (Mark 8:33; NIV).

So within Scripture the boundaries of how we express "good disagreement" do not always fall where we might expect. Some of this can be explained – as with Martin Luther – by setting these specific examples in their wider literary context and also the culture of the time and its particular standards and patterns of rhetoric and polemic, which are different from our own. There is, however, an important principle driving such strong approaches to disagreement. It is one to which we perhaps give less attention in our postmodern context where pluralism and relativism are such powerful forces: gospel truth matters and is a blessing to the world, so should be defended against errors that obscure the gospel and can be seriously detrimental for people's spiritual health. Error is dangerous and needs to be strenuously resisted and named for what it is – a powerful force that opposes the God of truth and threatens to damage the life and mission of the church.

In his classic study *Christ the Controversialist* John Stott writes:

> *In our generation we seem to have moved a long way from this vigorous passion for the truth displayed by Christ and his apostles. But if we loved the glory of God more, and if we cared more for the eternal good of other people, we would surely be more ready to engage in controversy when the truth of the gospel is at stake. The command is clear. We are to "maintain the truth in love" [Ephesians 4:15] – being neither truthless in our love, nor loveless in our truth, but holding the two in balance.[3]*

The apostle Paul also warns us to have nothing to do with "foolish and stupid arguments because you know they produce quarrels" (2 Timothy 2:23; NIV), on which Stott comments:

> *There's something wrong with us if we relish controversy… Controversy conducted in a hostile way, which descends to personal insult and abuse, stains all too many of the pages of church history. But we cannot avoid controversy itself. "Defending and confirming the gospel" [Philippians 1:7] is part of what God calls us to do.[4]*

Nevertheless, this passion for truth must always be deeply imbued with grace, because Jesus Christ himself embodies both grace and truth (John 1:14). The letters of the apostle Paul, despite his reputation for straight-talking, are also shot through with grace and gentleness. He is clear that there are ways of disagreeing and patterns of conflict which, although they arise among believers, have no place in the Christian community. To the Galatians he warns that "if you bite and devour each other, watch out or you will be destroyed by each other"; and counsels that "if someone is caught in a sin, you who live by the Spirit should restore that person gently" (Galatians 5:15; 6:1; NIV). Similarly in Philippians his attack upon opponents in chapter 3 is sandwiched between a call for the church to imitate the humility of Christ (chapter 2) and a plea to two Christian women, Euodia and Syntyche, to put their disagreement aside and "be of the same mind in the Lord", calling on the wider church to help them in doing this (chapter 4). In Romans, Paul calls on believers to "accept the one whose faith is weak, without quarrelling over disputable matters". In response to these disagreements he asks, "Who are you to judge someone else's servant?" and urges, "Let us therefore make every effort to do what leads to peace and to mutual edification" (Romans 14:1, 4, 19; NIV). He exhorts the Ephesians to live in a manner worthy of their Christian calling, "with all humility and gentleness, with patience, bearing with one another in love, eager to maintain the unity of the Spirit in the bond of peace" (Ephesians 4:2–3; ESV).

In his final letters, preparing the next generation of leaders, Paul remains clear on the imperative to uphold and defend the truth, but also the need for care in handling and distinguishing between different types of disagreement. Grace and gentleness remain a keynote. To Titus, he writes that believers should be "peaceable and considerate, always gentle toward everyone" (Titus 3:2; NIV). To Timothy he gives similar instructions:

The Lord's servant must not be quarrelsome but must be kind to everyone, able to teach, not resentful. Opponents must be gently

instructed, in the hope that God will grant them repentance leading
them to a knowledge of the truth, and that they will come to their senses
and escape from the trap of the devil, who has taken them captive to do
his will. (2 Timothy 2:24–26; NIV)

Timothy is told to pursue both "righteousness" and "gentleness" (1 Timothy 6:11). Patience and gentleness are both part of the fruit of the Holy Spirit (Galatians 5:22–23), and reflect the character of God who "is patient with you, not wanting anyone to perish, but everyone to come to repentance" (2 Peter 3:9; NIV).

A biblical approach to "good disagreement" in the contemporary church needs to hold together these different strands of the New Testament witness. When Christians are shaken by the disagreements that sometimes drive at the heart of belief and discipleship, can we hold firmly to a life of both grace and truth? Of righteousness and gentleness? What does that look like in practice?

Agreeing to disagree

Faced with disagreements in the church, Christians frequently polarize into two camps, one stressing "truth" and the other stressing "grace". The first camp rejects the possibility of maintaining fellowship across our disagreements, insisting that the only proper response is continued disputation, defending truth, combatting error, and some degree of division or separation. The second camp claims that Christian agreement is unobtainable, perhaps even undesirable. Instead it welcomes diverse views and practices within the church, to be tolerated and perhaps even celebrated, often with the motto "*Let's agree to disagree*".

"Agreeing to disagree" is not a postmodern, relativist invention, but has a long Christian heritage. George Whitefield, the eighteenth-century evangelist, was an ecumenist at heart. An Anglican by ordination and inclination, he travelled thousands of miles across Britain and North America preaching the Christian message to vast crowds and building gospel partnership with a wide variety of churches, including Baptists, Presbyterians, and Congregationalists. Provided the gospel was central, Whitefield was willing to lay aside questions of secondary importance over the sacraments, or episcopal authority, or church and state relations. As he wrote to a correspondent in 1750: "those that will live in peace must agree to disagree in many things with their fellow-labourers, and not let little things part or disunite them".[5]

Whitefield and his friend John Wesley disagreed over important doctrinal issues, chiefly concerning the sovereignty and grace of God, and sometimes they fell out with each other. Nonetheless, in an act of rapprochement, Whitefield asked Wesley to preach his funeral sermon, which was delivered in London in November 1770. Wesley exhorted the congregation to unite around "the grand scriptural doctrines" which Whitefield had preached across the globe, principally the seriousness of sin, justification "by faith alone" in Jesus Christ, and "new birth" by the power of the Holy Spirit. But Wesley continued:

> *There are many doctrines of a less essential nature, with regard to which, even the sincere children of God (such is the present weakness of human understanding!) are and have been divided for many ages. In these we may think and let think; we may "agree to disagree". But mean time let us hold fast the essentials of the faith, which was once delivered to the saints; and which this champion of God so strongly insisted on, at all times, and in all places.[6]*

The revivalists aimed to model this principle of unity in essentials and gracious disagreement on non-essentials.

Nevertheless, "agreeing to disagree" cannot be a universal panacea to resolve all disputes between Christians. Some have interpreted it as another way of saying that doctrine doesn't matter, and that a plurality of competing and contradictory theologies can be held together in the same church. Henry Dowson, a Baptist minister in Bradford, noticed this trend and protested to the Baptist Tract Society in 1851:

> *I know it is a favourite maxim of the present day; we hear it reiterated*
> *on all sides,* let us agree to differ; *but I cannot agree to differ. If a*
> *man holds error, I must differ from him; but I cannot* agree *to differ;*
> *there must be* separation, *where the truth of Christ is involved.*
> *Christian union is permanent, and sound only, when founded upon*
> *truth and Christian principles.[7]*

The crucial task is to identify those foundational truths. If all views are embraced within the church, then it has ceased to take seriously its calling to be a witness to truth and righteousness and to have a distinct identity as the body of Christ in the world. Sometimes that means refusing to "agree to disagree". The twentieth century provides prominent examples of Christians very determinedly rejecting error in the face of major pressure from their wider societies while a large number of fellow Christians were being carried along by the cultural tide. Most famous is Dietrich Bonhoeffer and the Confessing Church standing out against German Protestants who accepted Aryan ideology under the Nazis. A similar witness was given by Christians in South Africa who fiercely opposed apartheid in the face of its defence by some Reformed denominations. Although not obvious to some in the church at the time, in retrospect these protests appear uncontroversial to us. On other occasions a stand has been taken by Christians which remains controversial, like the Christian pacifists unable to remain in denominations that accept "just war" theology, who have formed separate "peace churches" as a witness to what they see as central to the gospel of peace.

Stott comments on errors in the church:

> *We need to make a distinction between the tolerant mind and the*
> *tolerant spirit. A Christian should always be tolerant in* spirit –
> *loving, understanding, forgiving and being patient with others, making*

> *allowances for them, and giving them the benefit of the doubt, for true*
> *love "always protects, always trusts, always hopes, always perseveres" [1*
> *Corinthians 13:7]. But how can we be tolerant in* mind *of what God*
> *has clearly revealed to be wrong?*[8]

Believers like Bonhoeffer identified a disputed matter in their own generation as a so-called *status confessionis* – a moment when they were called to stand up and confess their allegiance to Christ (Matthew 10:32) – and refused to "agree to disagree". They instead offered a prophetic witness by insisting that "disagreement" was, in reality, a cloak for "disobedience" to the Word of God. The church is called to obey God and to call all people to the "obedience of faith" (a kind of *inclusio* in Paul's letter to the Romans – Romans 1:5; 16:26). There is no such thing as "good disobedience".[9]

When offered as a universal solution for all disputes, "agreeing to disagree" is fatally flawed. But to reject it outright as never appropriate makes the same fundamental error. Although this looks like the exact opposite strategy, it is in fact its mirror image: a mistaken insistence that all disagreements between Christians be treated in the same way, with the same blunt tools, regardless of the subject. Instead, the church must undertake the difficult task of distinguishing between disagreements and making discriminating judgments in response.

John Wesley, in advocating (in contrast to Dowson) the rightness of agreeing to disagree, was following a principle which the Evangelical Revival as a whole aimed to model, though it has to be admitted not always with success: unity in essentials and "good disagreement" on non-essentials. This approach is encapsulated in the great ecumenical motto for peacemakers in the church, *in necessariis unitas, in dubiis libertas, in omnibus caritas*, which loosely translates as "in essentials unity, on doubtful matters freedom, in all things love". Coined in the seventeenth century, it was popularized by Richard Baxter, a puritan minister at Kidderminster in Worcestershire, whose ecumenical vision was forged in the deeply divisive context of the English civil wars.[10] He modelled ecumenism when others embraced conflict, and he pursued the purity and unity of the church in equal measure. The motto has endured because of its wise distinction that some doctrines matter more than others, and that whether Christians agree or disagree all their relationships must be deeply imbued with love and grace. Charles Wesley set it to music in his hymn, in *The Methodist Hymnal*, on 1 Corinthians 13:

> *Let all hold fast the truths whereby*
> *A church must stand or fall;*
> *In doubtful things grant liberty,*
> *Show charity in all.*
> *Thus shall we to our sacred name*
> *Our title clearly prove,*
> *While even our enemies exclaim,*
> *"See how these Christians love."*

Wesley here echoes Tertullian, the third-century Christian apologist who imagined pagans looking with admiration at the radical relationships within the church and saying in wonder: "See, how they love one another and are ready even to die for each other" (*Apology* 39.7).

In dubiis libertas is an important Christian principle. When the Bible is clear in its teaching, the church must insist upon it.[11] But sometimes the Bible is not clear, and there is legitimate room for debate among Christians. Creedal confessions always have to navigate this path between gospel certainties and subjects of doubt. For example, when Archbishop Thomas Cranmer was drawing up a statement of belief for the Church of England in the 1550s, he included an article (based on a particular reading of 1 Peter 3:19) which declared that between the crucifixion and the resurrection, while the body of Jesus lay in the tomb, the spirit of Jesus preached to the spirits in hell. But the Elizabethan bishops in the next generation decided it was wrong to bind the consciences of ministers on such disputable points, when Scripture was obscure or open to a variety of interpretations. They therefore deleted Cranmer's words to allow liberty on this question. They did the same for his article about whether the souls of the departed sleep until the Day of Judgment.[12] These things may have been clear to the Archbishop of Canterbury, but they were not clear to the whole church.

This freedom to disagree need not mean doctrinal pluralism and relativism in disguise. The key question is whether our disagreements are over matters which are of foundational importance for the Christian gospel and Christian discipleship. In that case, there must be a clear determination and separation from error – as, for example, the early church discovered in the arguments between Athanasius and Arius concerning the deity of Christ, hammered out at the Council of Nicaea in the fourth century. But if what is at stake is not of foundational importance, then disagreement is permitted within the church, and "agreeing to disagree" is laudable in order that we can focus our energies on partnership in living and preaching the gospel.

This means, of course, that it is of critical importance to distinguish, on a case by case basis, between different areas of disagreement. The Second Vatican Council stated: "When comparing doctrines with one another, they [Catholic theologians] should remember that in Catholic doctrine there exists an order or 'hierarchy' of truths, since they vary in their relation to the foundation of the Christian faith."[13] Other theologians prefer to speak of "core doctrines" and *adiaphora* (matters indifferent); or of primary, secondary, and tertiary issues. This opens up another level of complexity, because two Christians may agree on the substance of an issue, but disagree on its significance, and thus respond in different ways (and perhaps even separate from each other as a result). What is clear is that the church often finds itself in a tangled mess when it fails to distinguish properly. To mistake non-essentials for essentials breeds needless division and separation; and to mistake essentials for non-essentials sacrifices the very gospel itself.

J.C. Ryle, an Anglican Bishop of Liverpool and a prominent evangelical spokesman, aimed to model "good disagreement" during the heated ecclesiastical disputes of the late nineteenth century. But he rejected the idea of unity "purchased at the expense of distinctive truth, and built on the ruins of creeds and doctrines". Disagreement in the church can, he argued, be a healthy reminder that truth matters:

Unity obtained in this worldly fashion, by throwing overboard all disputed points, and ordering the clergy to practise a kind of doctrinal teetotalism, is simply worthless and absurd... Better a thousand times for Churchmen to disagree and be alive, than to exhibit a dumb show of unity and be dead...[14]

Controversy and disagreement in the church is not simply a curse. It can be a blessing in disguise because it forces us to go back to the Bible with renewed diligence and prayer, to clarify the issues at stake. A general policy of "agreeing to disagree" runs the risk of persuading the church to settle too easily for disagreement as a permanent fact of life, as if we will never be able to judge rightly between the many contradictory interpretations of the Bible so should give up trying. Rather we need to settle our disagreements at the bar of Scripture, listening to the voice of God speaking his words of grace to us.

"Good disagreement" in contemporary debate

In the last few years, the language of "good disagreement" has risen to prominence as a key for Christian relationships, due particularly to the theological leadership of the Archbishop of Canterbury, Justin Welby. His predecessor, Rowan Williams, invested considerable energies in seeking some basis for theological agreement between divided churches, for example through an Anglican Communion Covenant, but with limited success. Archbishop Welby has highlighted disagreement as an indelible fact of life, as he explained on BBC Radio 4 in January 2014: "It's not exactly startling that we have disagreements. What I'm trying to do is not to get everyone to agree – because I don't think we're going to agree – it is to try to transform bad disagreement to good disagreement."[15] This has brought a fresh emphasis on the need for reconciliation in the contemporary church (one of the priorities of the archbishop's ministry), and rekindled hopes that a breakthrough is possible in navigating our disagreements in a divided church.

Unlike most British church leaders, the archbishop has extensive personal experience of ministry in war zones and other conflict situations, including Iraq, Israel, Nigeria, Kenya, Burundi, and elsewhere. His passion for reconciliation between Christians is forged in a context of warring tribes and community violence. The purpose of reconciliation in those contexts, he explains, is not to resolve conflict or end disagreement, but to enable enemies and opponents "to continue to disagree without violence or mutual destruction".[16] Speaking at the New Wine Conference, he drew a distinction between reconciliation and the end of argument: "Reconciliation is conflict transformed, not concluded. It's conflict with words, not with AK47s." Or again, "Conflict itself is not bad, it's only bad when it gets out of control."[17]

After decades of acrimonious theological wrangling, the Church of England's General Synod finally approved legislation in July 2014 for the consecration of women to the episcopate. The debates had been marked on all sides by *odium theologicum*, violent language, broken relationships, pride, suspicion, and grief. But rather than throw out the defeated minority, the final settlement aimed to hold Anglicans together in one ecclesial body, despite their sharp disagreements over this subject. The archbishop turned to a favourite metaphor of the church as family, brothers and sisters in Christ, when he promised General Synod: "You do not chuck out family or even make it difficult for them to be at home. You love them and seek their well-being, even when you disagree."[18] He spoke of his delight that a way through the impasse had been found at last:

> *Today marks the start of a great adventure of seeking mutual flourishing while still, in some cases, disagreeing. The challenge for us*

will be for the church to model good disagreement and to continue to demonstrate love for those who disagree on theological grounds. Very few institutions achieve this, but if we manage this we will be living out more fully the call of Jesus Christ to love one another.[19]

"Good disagreement", in this sense, is a sign of the transformative power of the gospel if the church, instead of behaving like secular society, can model disagreement with grace, eschewing violence, bitterness, and one-upmanship, and keeping the family together. To the National Parliamentary Press Breakfast, the archbishop reiterated: "We do not have the option, if we love one another, of simply ditching those with whom we disagree." He called for Christians to pioneer "a radical new way of being the Church" where "good and loving disagreement" is

a potential gift to a world of bitter and divisive conflict. What can be more radical than to disagree well, not by abandoning principle and truth, but affirming it – agreeing what is right, acting on it and yet continuing to love those who have a different view?

In a global church, embracing thousands of cultures with a multitude of nations and languages, the ability to hold together in good disagreement "sets a pattern in which truth is not a club with which to strike others, but a light freely offered for a path of joy and flourishing".[20]

The language of "good disagreement" has been applied not just to questions of church order (e.g. men and women in ministry), but also to weightier questions of doctrine and morals (e.g. marriage and sexuality). For example, according to the archbishop, the process of formal Church of England Conversations about sexuality during 2015–16 "has at its heart a search for good disagreement".[21] Likewise the College of Bishops acknowledged that there were "strongly held and divergent views" among Anglicans and that "we will not all agree", but they were "committed to seeking good disagreement that testifies to our love for one another across the church in obedience to Christ".[22] The formal guidelines for the Conversations reiterated:

> *There is no expectation of achieving any consensus – in either direction – in the foreseeable future. But there is a task to be done of encouraging those within the church who are at odds on this issue to express their concerns in a safe environment, listen carefully to those with whom they disagree profoundly, find something of Christ in each other and consider together what the practical consequence of disagreement might be.[23]*

The way the church handles this debate has major implications for its public witness. Therefore one question asks, "Recognising the fact of profound disagreement within the church, can we find a way together to make the manner of our encounter with each other a gift to a broken world, and not a scandal?"[24]

One of the challenges is that "good disagreement" has not been clearly defined. It is a highly flexible and permeable concept, meaning different things to different people. At one level, it is impossible to dissent from it. No one wants to recommend "bad disagreement" instead! Nevertheless, some argue that the whole idea is fundamentally flawed because disagreement is a result of human sin and ignorance since the Fall and we disagree with each other because we are blind to the truth or deliberately reject it. From this perspective, "good disagreement" is an oxymoron like "virtuous sin", and the church should be known as a place where the truth is discerned, accepted, and celebrated. There will be no disagreements in heaven and so, it is argued, the church is called to testify to that reality.[25]

Others are happy to embrace the language of "good disagreement" if it means disagreeing with grace, or disagreeing "Christianly". Here the focus is primarily upon the development of Christian character, so that our disputes may be handled in ways that are more godly and more winsome. Bishop Ryle, quoted earlier, was a strong advocate for properly distinguishing the essential and non-essential aspects of the Christian gospel as the bedrock for unity. Concerning the *non necessaria* he urged courteous tolerance for diversity of opinion and practice (in typically Victorian language):

> *Nothing, I am convinced, divides and keeps Churchmen apart so much as the common habit of getting hot, and calling names, and throwing mud, and casting dust in the air about non-essentials... I do protest against the common practice of ramping and raging and using violent language about matters which neither exclude a man from heaven nor from the Church of England... For Christ's sake let us all try to give up this wretched, narrow, illiberal practice of savagely condemning, anathematising, and even excommunicating our brethren about things indifferent. Let us try to disagree pleasantly, civilly, and like Christian gentlemen.*

To foster such good disagreement, Ryle gave three further pieces of wise practical advice. First, cultivate the habit of recognizing the grace of God and love for Jesus Christ, wherever that grace and love are found, sometimes in the most surprising places. Second, grab opportunities to meet with Christians from other sections of the church as often as possible, to help "rub off corners and lessen prejudices". "Nothing is more common", Ryle mourned, "than to find one Churchman disliking another, without ever having seen his face, heard his voice, or read one line of his writings!" Third, cooperate with other Christians wherever possible.[26] Good disagreement, in this sense, means "better quality disagreement" which is imbued with grace.

More contentious, though, is another interpretation of "good disagreement" which highlights how the concept can be shaped in different ways to suit different theological agendas. In the diocese of Oxford, for example, the bishop's staff team developed the idea in the following fashion, in answer to the question "What does good disagreement look like?":

> *It's unrealistic to expect everyone to be brought to a single position on same-sex relationships. What we can look for, however, is a way of living with disagreement that honours and respects views we don't agree with, believing that those who hold such views are not just perverse, ignorant or immoral, but rather are bearing witness to different aspects of the truth that lies in Christ alone. Not only is all truth God's truth, but God's truth is ultimately bound to be beyond our grasp because our minds are but miniscule receptors before the great and beautiful Mystery of God.*[27]

This statement begins with the indisputable fact that agreement is unlikely and urges that disagreement be respectful. It then, however, makes a major theological leap which many would consider doubtful. It argues that we should "respect" and "honour" not only the other person but also their views. This fails to make a key distinction – that not every view held by a Christian is necessarily a legitimate Christian view: some of our opinions may be sub-Christian, or even anti-Christian, and in need of correction. Furthermore the statement presumes that all these views bear witness in some sense to the truth found in Christ, without any reference to their content.

These rival interpretations of "good disagreement" expose the complexities and ambiguities of the concept. Does it mean welcoming contradictory views as good and godly, and as all parts of God's truth? Or does it mean disagreeing firmly but graciously, insisting that the other person is in serious error and that, rather than incorporating their views, the church needs to call on them to change their mind or even to repent?

If, as we have argued, each dispute within the church needs to be carefully examined in its own right before we determine its practical consequences for our common life and gospel witness, then "good disagreement" must allow for situations where "agreeing to disagree" cannot be justified. Broadly speaking, most Christians accept that there are issues of doctrine (e.g. the uniqueness of Christ and redemption only through him) and ethics (e.g. the rejection of injustice and sexual immorality) which are more important than issues of ecclesiastical order (e.g. ordination and infant baptism) because they reach to the heart of the good news about salvation. Applying the language of "good disagreement" in an identical way to all disputed questions, as if they are equivalent, leads to confusion and fails to distinguish their relative importance. On some issues, "good disagreement" will mean renewed efforts to hold together despite the inevitable strains. On other issues, it may require discipline, differentiation, or even some form of separation among professing Christians – in which case its "goodness" will be evident by the continuing witness to God's grace and truth in how we walk apart: in humility and sorrow, with blessing not cursing, with gentleness not venom. Whether "good disagreement" means holding together or walking apart, the church has a precious opportunity to witness to a watching world that bitter conflicts can be transformed for good when the gospel of grace takes centre stage.

This book

The purpose of this book is to examine the idea of "good disagreement" from a number of different angles: biblical, historical, theological, and practical. The team of authors are all Anglicans, but we write for the wider church, not just for our own denomination. We have purposefully avoided trying to address or resolve specific disputes, and the authors disagree among themselves on a number of matters. Our intention, rather, is to lay out a broad framework, and practical reflections, to help Christian readers who are seeking to discern what "good disagreement" looks like in their own situations and their own churches.

The following chapters begin with an exploration of the New Testament witness. Ian Paul examines the meaning of "reconciliation", especially in the Pauline letters, and Michael Thompson surveys the apostolic injunctions about division and church discipline. Tom Wright then unpacks how the apostle Paul held together a passion for unity and a passion for holiness, and how the church can distinguish between differences that matter and differences that don't. Ashley Null analyses Reformation disagreements, and Andrew Atherstone and Martin Davie survey the work of Christian ecumenism.

The final four chapters are personal reflections which draw upon the authors' varied experiences of seeking "good disagreement" in different contemporary contexts. Toby Howarth provides lessons from interfaith dialogue in England, while Lis Goddard and Clare Hendry reflect on their conversations about the role of women in Christian leadership. Tory Baucum writes as rector of a parish in Virginia, which, having separated from The Episcopal Church and been embroiled in acrimonious litigation, now has a peacemaking and bridge-building ministry. Finally, Stephen Ruttle describes his own journey as a mediator, explaining how the resolution of conflict and disagreement is good news both within and outside the church.

***

A few questions are supplied by the editors after every chapter, for personal reflection or small group discussion.

Questions

1. Have you ever disagreed badly with a fellow Christian? Why did this happen, and could it have been handled differently?

2. How do you react to the strong words of rebuke by Jesus and the apostles in the New Testament? What implications do they have for "good disagreement" today?

3. What does it mean in practice to respond to disagreements with both grace and truth?

4. When have you felt able, or unable, to "agree to disagree" with another Christian?

5. What criteria help us distinguish between "essentials" and "*adiaphora*"?

2
Reconciliation in the New Testament
Ian Paul

Is disagreement among Christians a contradiction of the good news of reconciliation? New Testament scholar Ian Paul examines the language of reconciliation in the apostle Paul's letters and its broader significance. He offers a synthesis of Pauline and Gospel teaching, showing how God takes the initiative to reconcile humanity to himself through Christ as an act of grace and a necessary precursor to reconciliation between divided people.

What does "reconciliation" mean?

As we consider the meaning of reconciliation in the New Testament, we need to think carefully about the words that are used. When translating from one language to another, there is never an exact match between the ranges of meaning in the two languages. So we need to go back to the source language, and the words used there, to have a real grasp of what reconciliation is about.

"Reconciliation" and "to reconcile" in English Bible versions translate the Greek words *diallassomai* (once), *sunallasso* (once), *katallasso* (six times) and its related noun *katallage* (four times), and *apokatallasso* (three times). It is worth, from the outset, highlighting a basic difference in the etymology of the English and Greek terms, which will become significant as we explore their use. "Reconciliation" is derived from the Latin *re-* (meaning "back") and *conciliare* (meaning "bring together"). Implicit in this is the movement of two parties, previously at a (metaphorical) distance from one another, so that they are now close to one another again. In this sense, the English term has a neutrality about it, where both sides can be seen as equal parties in the movement.[1]

One of the Greek terms used, *sunallasso*, has a similar sense, in that the prefix *sun-* means "together". But the most commonly used words (*katallasso, katallage, apokatallasso*) have quite a different derivation and as a result have a quite different sense to them. The two elements *kata* and *allos* originally mean "according to another", so early uses of these terms simply have the sense of change or exchange, similar to the non-compound *allasso* (this occurs in Romans 1:23, 1 Corinthians 15:51, Galatians 4:20, and Hebrews 1:12 and is translated "exchange" or "change"). The first-century biographer Plutarch, writing in similar Greek to that of the New Testament, uses *katallasso* for the exchange of money (*Life of Aratus*, 18). The historian Dio Cassius, writing a little later, uses it for an exchange of prisoners (*Roman Histories* 16.57.36). But it has also been used to mean a change in a person's status; some centuries earlier, the historian Herodotus used it in the sense of someone changing from being an enemy to being a friend (*Histories* 5.29), and this is reflected in some English translations of the term in the New Testament. So whereas the English word "reconciliation" emphasizes coming together – and from that we might infer that the parties have changed from enemies to friends – the Greek term focuses first on the change of status, and only from that might we infer a coming together.

The fifteen occurrences come in four groups of texts with four emphases: (1) reconciliation between individuals; (2) reconciliation as salvation; (3) reconciliation as the aim of Christian ministry; (4) reconciliation as the goal of the cosmos.

Reconciliation between individuals

Therefore, if you are offering your gift at the altar and there remember that your brother or sister has something against you, leave your gift there in front of the altar. First go and **be reconciled** *to that person; then come and offer your gift. (Matthew 5:23–24; NIV)*

The next day Moses came upon two Israelites who were fighting. He tried to **reconcile** *them by saying, "Men, you are brothers; why do you want to hurt each other?" (Acts 7:26; NIV)*

To the married I give this command (not I, but the Lord): A wife must not separate from her husband. But if she does, she must remain unmarried or else **be reconciled** *to her husband. And a husband must not divorce his wife. (1 Corinthians 7:10–11; NIV)*

In these three examples, reconciliation is not between God and people, but between different individuals. The first, in Matthew 5, has the closest connection to relationship with God. Because God is judge of all, I cannot be reconciled with God through my offering as long as I have caused offence to another, so I must go and be reconciled with that person first. So, although the language of reconciliation is here between two individuals, the impulse towards human reconciliation has been set in motion by the desire to be at peace with God and be able to make the offering with a clear conscience. Note the assumption here that the one who has caused the offence is the one who initiates reconciliation. This is even clearer in the saying that follows in Matthew 5:25. In Matthew's version of the saying, Jesus urges us to "settle matters" with the one who has a case against us; in Luke's version (12:58, set in a different context in Jesus' teaching) some English translations render this as "be reconciled" with the one taking you to court.

The use in Acts 7:26 of *sunallasso* reflects Moses' attempt to bring together two warring compatriots. The language of reconciliation is not present in the Exodus account itself (Exodus 2:13) but expresses Luke's (or Stephen's) view of Moses as an exemplary sage.[2] Wise leaders of God's people seek to bring an end to conflict.

In 1 Corinthians 7, Anthony Thiselton notes both the mutuality and symmetry of the instruction to men and women, and its dependence on Jesus' teaching about marriage and divorce in Mark 10:9–12.[3]

Reconciliation as salvation (Romans)

> *For if, while we were God's enemies, we were* **reconciled** *to him through the death of his Son, how much more, having been* **reconciled**, *shall we be saved through his life! Not only is this so, but we also boast in God through our Lord Jesus Christ, through whom we have now received* **reconciliation**. *(Romans 5:10–11; NIV)*

> *For if their rejection brought* **reconciliation** *to the world, what will their acceptance be but life from the dead? (Romans 11:15)*

There is some debate on whether chapter 5 in Romans belongs with Paul's argument in chapters 1–4 or belongs with chapters 6–8. Either way, this passage is part of a key transition from the problem humanity faces to the solution that God in Christ offers. In the immediate verses (6–11) there are a series of parallels:

> ... *while we were weak... Christ died for the ungodly... (6)*
> ... *while we were still sinners, Christ died for us... (8)*
> ... *we have been justified by his blood, much more surely will we be saved... (9)*
> ... *while we were enemies, we were reconciled to God through the death of his Son, much more surely will we be saved... (10)*

The effect of this is to clarify the status of humanity before God – we were weak, we were ungodly, we were enemies. But it also puts "reconciliation" in parallel with justification (Paul appears to use these almost interchangeably) and makes clear how such reconciliation is effected, by the death of Jesus on the cross. In Romans 5 there are more mentions of Christ and his death than in any other part of Paul's writing,[4] and three of the fifteen New Testament occurrences of the terms for "reconciliation" come here.

This all makes the theme of change of status clear and prominent: we *were* God's enemies, but we have now been changed – by implication, into friends of God. There is a further parallel from the beginning of the chapter: "since we are justified... we have peace with God through our Lord Jesus Christ" (verse 1). Jesus' death justifies us; that is, reconciles us with God by changing us from enemies of God so that we now have peace with God. It might be argued that this reconciliation is objective and declared, but Paul also implies that at the same time it is subjective and experienced; our confidence stems in part from "the love of God poured into our hearts by the Holy Spirit" (verse 5).

It is worth noting the lack of symmetry in the use here of "reconciliation" language. Whereas reconciliation is elsewhere assumed to be initiated by the party who caused the offence, here it is initiated by the one who has been offended – God himself. In other uses, the change of status that comes about is a change in both parties; their mutual status has changed from "enemies" to "friends". But here Paul's language is quite one-sided; it is we who were the "enemies", and it is our status that has been changed into that of "friends". This corresponds with Paul's one-sided use of the term "reconcile"; it is always we who are reconciled to God, and not God who is reconciled to us. God is the active agent in reconciling humanity to himself.

The occurrence of the term in Romans 11 suggests that Paul is happy to use it as an overarching term for the whole process of salvation, and that it has cosmic significance ("reconciliation to the *world*").

Reconciliation as the aim of Christian ministry (2 Corinthians)

> *All this is from God, who* **reconciled** *us to himself through Christ and gave us the ministry of* **reconciliation**: *that God was* **reconciling** *the world to himself in Christ, not counting people's sins against them. And he has committed to us the message of* **reconciliation**. *We are therefore Christ's ambassadors, as though God were making his appeal through us. We implore you on Christ's behalf:* **Be reconciled** *to God. (2 Corinthians 5:18–20; NIV)*

This is the most extensive theological reflection by Paul on the notion of reconciliation, including five of the fifteen New Testament occurrences of "reconcile", and in it he makes a number of key assertions.

First, the immediate context links reconciliation to the eschatological idea of "new creation" in verse 17. For Paul, Jesus' death and resurrection bring about the start of the longed-for "new age". The life that Christians live now is a first taste of the transformation that the whole world will experience on Jesus' return (see Romans 8:18–23). This then relates "reconciliation" to the cosmic vision of "the restoration of all things" (Matthew 17:11; Acts 3:21), which is pictured in Revelation 7:9 as a multitude from every nation, tribe, people, and language gathered before the throne of God and singing his praise with one voice. The reconciliation we experience between ourselves as a result of our reconciliation with God points towards the eschatological unity of humankind that God longs for as the end point and goal of creation. This explains the "universal" language in both 2 Corinthians 5 and Romans 5 ("all have died", "all will be made alive"). In Christ, God was reconciling the *world* to himself (the same cosmic language as in Romans 11:15).

Second, it is clear that the one doing the reconciling is God. He is the active agent and we are the objects, the passive recipients of his reconciling activity. Paul's plea to the Christians in Corinth is to "be reconciled" by the reconciling work of God. It is also clear that this reconciliation is not, in the first instance, between people, but between each person and God – in fact, it is striking that Paul does not here make the link between our reconciliation to God and our reconciliation to one another which must inevitably follow. The asymmetry of the language, between we who are reconciled and God as the one doing the reconciling, provides a powerful parallel to that in Romans 5. Together, these two passages provide the first example in any Greek text of the person who is doing the reconciling also being the offended party to whom the other is reconciled. In other examples, the two parties are mutually reconciled, sometimes by a third party, or the offender initiates the process of reconciliation, as you would expect. But here, God, the offended party, is the one who takes the initiative.[5] This is through and through the language of grace – our reconciliation owes nothing to our own action and initiative, but is a gift of grace from God to be received freely.

It is also striking here that Paul uses reconciliation as a comprehensive description of his ministry. Elsewhere he talks of his ministry as one of proclamation (Romans 10:14); or of teaching and handing on the "tradition" (*paradosis*, 1 Corinthians 15:1–11). But in 2 Corinthians he is an ambassador of the gospel, appealing to his audience to receive this costly, cosmic initiative of reconciliation offered to them through the cross and resurrection of Jesus. This has important implications for what it means to be part of the "one, holy, catholic, and *apostolic* church". To follow in Paul's apostolic footprints will involve, at times, proclamation and teaching. But the calling of the people of God is encapsulated by the idea of our being God's ambassadors, reasoning and pleading with the world, urging it to receive this gift of reconciliation to God, being changed from enemies to friends with God.

Reconciliation as the goal of the cosmos (Ephesians and Colossians)

For he himself is our peace, who has made the two one and has destroyed the barrier, the dividing wall of hostility, by setting aside in his flesh the law with its commands and regulations. His purpose was to create in himself one new humanity out of the two, thus making peace, and in one body to **reconcile** *both of them to God through the cross, by which he put to death their hostility. He came and preached peace to you who were far away and peace to those who were near. For through him we both have access to the Father by one Spirit. (Ephesians 2:14–18; NIV)*

For God was pleased to have all his fullness dwell in him, and through him to **reconcile** *to himself all things, whether things on earth or things in heaven, by making peace through his blood, shed on the cross. Once you were alienated from God and were enemies in your minds because of your evil behaviour. But now he has* **reconciled** *you by Christ's physical body through death to present you holy in his sight, without blemish and free from accusation. (Colossians 1:19–21; NIV)*

These texts offer a further perspective on the nature of reconciliation. Like Romans 5, Ephesians 2 emphasizes peace with God as the result of reconciliation, which brings us into relationship with God despite our previous situation. Again, reconciliation is in the first instance "to God", and only secondarily (though indispensably) between the two groups, Jews and Gentiles. Since the reconciliation is to God, the "hostility" (*echthra*, verse 16) which was "put to death" on the cross must be the hostility of both groups to God.[6] And yet the "dividing wall of hostility" (verse 14) is Paul's reference to the partition wall separating Jews and Gentiles in the Jerusalem Temple as a metaphor for the function of the law (Torah) which kept them apart. So it is clear that, with the ending of hostilities towards God, hostilities between these two groups also come to an end.

The importance of reconciliation between these two parties is very striking. Paul goes so far as to say that the "purpose" or "goal" of God's plan of redemption was to create "one new humanity, making peace". He is clear that this cannot happen without reconciliation to God, but also clear that peace and reconciliation between God's people is an inevitable consequence. If we are not reconciled with one another, this is evidence that we have not been reconciled to God.

This could be seen to function as a summary statement for what Paul says in other ways elsewhere. In his criticism of the Corinthian "party spirit", Paul's first challenge is, "Has Christ been divided?" (1 Corinthians 1:13; NRSV). There should be no divisions, but unity, since we are one body in Christ. This is connected to the unity of God in both 1 Corinthians and Ephesians: there is "one God... and one Lord" (1 Corinthians 8:6); there is "one body, one Spirit... one hope... one Lord, one faith, one baptism, one God" (Ephesians 4:3–4). "In the one Spirit we were all baptized into one body – Jews or Greeks, slaves or free – and we were all made to drink of one Spirit" (1 Corinthians 12:13; NRSV).

True reconciliation between people cannot happen before reconciliation with God, who in the cross has destroyed the things that cause enmity both with God and between people. Conversely, reconciliation with God must lead to reconciliation between people, since God "is a God of peace" (1 Corinthians 14:33). In that sense, reconciliation and peace among God's people is testimony to our reconciliation with God in Christ.

The similar text in Colossians also mentions "making peace" and is slightly closer to Romans 5 in describing us as "enemies" rather than referring to "enmity". The perspective here is not on the Jew–Gentile relationship, but on the cosmic vision of the reconciliation and restoration of all things. The focus is more exclusively "upward", in that Paul talks of reconciliation to God effecting holiness (more clearly than in any part of Romans), without mentioning explicitly the consequences for relations between Christians. There is perhaps an echo of Romans 8:1 ("no condemnation for those who are in Christ Jesus") in the idea of being "free from accusation".

Reconciliation within Paul's theology

All this presents us with a puzzle. The occurrences of the term "reconciliation" are relatively few in Paul's letters, but they appear to have great significance within the shape of Paul's theology. How do we make sense of this? Ralph Martin proposes five criteria for discerning the centre of Paul's theology:

• the primacy of God's grace

• the cosmic significance of what God has done in Christ

• the centrality of the cross (and, we might add, resurrection)

• ethical imperative – the move from the indicative to the imperative, from what God has done in Christ to how Christians should then live

• the missionary mandate.

Reconciliation, more than any other term, meets these criteria for being the centre of Paul's theology. Martin writes:

> *It is the overall theme of reconciliation… that meets most – if not all – these tests. This is not to say that the word-group* katallass- *is prominent in Paul's writings; manifestly it is not… But the contention stands, namely, that reconciliation provides a suitable umbrella under which the main features of Paul's kerygma and its practical outworking may be set.*[7]

If this is the case, it is then less surprising that Tom Wright should introduce his *magnum opus* on Paul's theology with a study of his letter to Philemon, which has not traditionally been put at the centre of Paul's thinking. But Wright justifies this in very similar terms to Martin.

Although Paul values freedom, he values the mutual reconciliation of those who "belong to the Messiah" as more important – indeed, as taking precedence over all other concerns. "Reconciliation is what mattered," Wright explains.[8]

> *The heart of it all… is* koinonia, *a "partnership" or "fellowship"*
> *which is not static but which enables the community of those who*
> *believe to grow together into a unity across the traditional divisions of*
> *the human race. This is a unity which is nothing other than the unity*
> *of Jesus Christ and his people, – the unity, indeed, which Jesus Christ*
> *has won for his people precisely by his identifying with them and so,*
> *through his death and resurrection, effecting reconciliation between*
> *them and God.[9]*

He goes on to describe Paul's understanding of reconciliation and the unity of those in Christ as an anticipation of the goal of all humanity as springing out of a Jewish worldview, but then creating a new worldview all of its own.[10]

If reconciliation is of central importance in understanding what God has done, we might then expect peace (the result of reconciliation) to have similar prominence. It is striking that in all his letters, Paul modifies the traditional greeting from "grace" to "grace *and peace*". Michael Gorman thinks this is no accident:

> *For Paul, the prophetically promised age of eschatological, messianic*
> *peace has arrived in the death and resurrection of Jesus the Messiah,*
> *an age characterized especially by reconciliation and nonviolence.[11]*

Alan Spence, in his fascinating study of the atonement in Paul, also puts peace at the centre of Paul's theology:

> *[I] offer a provisional, highly condensed answer to the question: Why*
> *did God become man? It takes the shape of a master-story, presenting*
> *in narrative form the concept that Jesus is Mediator:* The Son

became as we are so that he might, on our behalf, make peace with God. *This is more than an account of individual forgiveness. It summarizes God's gracious intention to reorder or reconstitute around himself the broken relationships of his suffering and alienated creation through the death of his Son and by the work of his Spirit.*[12]

Reconciliation in the Gospels

If reconciliation is such a significant term in Paul, do we see this in the Gospels and in the ministry of Jesus?

One of the striking things about the narratives of Jesus' healings and deliverances is the way that restoration to wholeness is frequently followed by restoration of relationships and communities. In the brief account of Jesus healing Simon Peter's mother-in-law (Mark 1:30–31), her restoration to her role in the household as host follows on from her physical healing. The man with a skin disease is likewise returned to his ritual community upon healing: he is instructed to make the ritual offering prescribed by Leviticus 14 as testimony to what God has done for him (Mark 1:40–44). The Gerasene demoniac, living on the outer fringes of human society when Jesus meets him, is not only delivered from demonic possession but is also restored to his own community: "Go home to your own people…" (literally, "to your household and your own", Mark 5:19).

This pattern is found across the Gospels. In the carefully structured account of the raising of a widow's son in Luke 7:11–17 (told in such a way as to echo Elijah's similar action in 1 Kings 17), Jesus' compassion stands at the numerical centre of the story – Luke has arranged his retelling to have the same number of words before "compassion" as after it, so that we notice how central it is.[13] The restoration is made explicit: at the end of the miracle story, Jesus gives the boy back to his mother (verse 15). In Jesus' conversation with the woman at the well in John 4, the timing of the encounter has a literary/theological significance. The woman can see plainly who

Jesus is in the broad light of day, in contrast to Nicodemus in the preceding chapter who still gropes with his questions in the evening twilight. But the episode also has a cultural/historical significance: her noontime trip to the well also speaks of social rejection and marginalization. Yet as soon as her eyes are opened as to who Jesus really is, she returns to the community that has rejected her with a passionate invitation: "Come, see a man who told me everything I ever did! Could this be the Messiah?" (John 4:29; NIV).[14]

This focus on the reconciling effect of Jesus' ministry, which brings people peace not only with God but with one another, is particularly evident in Luke's writings. In his Gospel, he frequently focuses on the entourage who travel with Jesus and support him, and in Acts he emphasizes the unity and cohesion of this new "Jesus movement". Gorman writes:

> *For Luke, the age of peace has also been inaugurated; for him it arrives not only in Christ's death and resurrection, but already in the birth, ministry, death, resurrection and exaltation of Jesus and in the gift of the Spirit. This new age is characterized by reconciliation and nonviolence, but also especially by justice characterized by status-reversal and inclusion… Jesus came to create a new people who would walk in the way of peace, and this also defines the Spirit-filled church, "the Way".[15]*

But what is equally striking in the Gospels is that this reconciliation and restoration of relationships also brings with it sharp division. The most demanding expression of this comes in Jesus' saying in Matthew 10:34–36:

> *Do not suppose that I have come to bring peace to the earth. I did not come to bring peace, but a sword. For I have come to turn a man against his father, a daughter against her mother, a daughter-in-law against her mother-in-law. Your enemies will be the members of your own household.*

Matthew locates this saying within a collection of Jesus' sayings and teaching that he has gathered together, as is his habit. (The parallel in Luke 12:51–53 sits with other sayings.) It therefore needs to be distinguished from the material earlier in the same chapter on future persecution (10:17–25, which has parallels in Matthew 24, Mark 13, and Luke 21). In other words, this "division" is not something unique to times of hardship; it is integral to our recognition of Jesus as God's anointed one. This is made clear both by the preceding saying (Matthew 10:32–33), which introduces the notion of sharp distinction between those who do and those who do not acknowledge Jesus, and the use of the saying from Micah 7:6, widely interpreted to relate to the time of the coming Messiah. The irony of this is brought out by Matthew setting this saying in the context of a mission which was to proclaim "peace", as Dick France observes:

> *Peacemaking is an essential part of the good life [Matthew 5:9]. But the way to peace is not the way of avoidance of conflict, and Jesus will be continuously engaged in robust controversy especially in chs 21–23, while his whole experience will be the opposite of a peaceful way of life. His followers can expect no less, and their mission to establish God's peaceful rule can be accomplished only by sharing his experience of conflict.*[16]

This paradox of reconciliation/peace and conflict/division is expressed in narrative form in the story of the prodigal son in Luke 15:11–32. Although this parable is often taken as the quintessential expression of the gospel of God's grace, there are some striking contrasts with the previous stories of "the lost" that precede it. The father, while anxiously straining to look for the return of his son (usually inferred from verse 20), does not actually follow after him to seek him as the shepherd searching for his lost sheep (verse 4) or the woman searching for her lost coin (verse 8). In fact, the son is only restored because he has "come to his senses" (verse 7) and begun the journey home. There is material loss for the father as well as loss of dignity (in his running, verse 20) and a forfeiting of his right to exact retribution on the son who, in asking for his share of the estate, was effectively wishing his father dead.

The parable does, however, match the pattern of reconciliation that we have already seen. Though the son expresses his desire to accept the consequences of his action, it is the father who absorbs the cost and thereby effects the restoration of relationship, highlighted by the gift of robe and ring (verse 22). And the second half of the story, the complaint of the elder son at his father's generosity and forgiveness, is integral to the whole even though it is often treated as an appendix to the main story. Luke has structured this as a close parallel to the situation of Jesus, as he makes clear in verses 1–2. The "tax-collectors and sinners" come near to listen to Jesus, while the Pharisees and scribes grumble about his acceptance of them; the younger son returns to the father and is accepted by him while the elder son stays in the field complaining. So the reconciliation that Jesus brings, at cost to himself, in breaking down division and forming a new, unified humanity, brings division between those who will accept this reconciliation and those who will not. Joel Green sees the parable characterized in precisely these terms:

> *[The younger son attempts] to reconstrue their relationship as one of master/hired hand – a definition at odds with his father's persistence in regarding him in filial terms. Accepting his status as son, he is reconciled to his father and restored as a member of the family… Will they [the scribes and Pharisees] identify with God's will and, having done so, join repentant sinners at the table?… Or, refusing to embrace God's gracious calculus, which works to include those who (re)turn to him, will they exclude themselves from the family of God?*[17]

The dynamics of reconciliation

We therefore see the following dynamics at work in the New Testament's exposition of reconciliation:

1. Reconciliation is primarily the work of God, and is primarily between God and humanity. It is enormously costly, but against all the cultural norms, in this relationship it is God, the offended party, who both takes the initiative and pays the cost.

2. The language of reconciliation and peacemaking is arguably of central importance in both Paul and the Gospels. The continuing mission of the apostolic church can be summed up as being ambassadors of God who plead with the world to be reconciled to God – to receive the gift of grace that is held out in the offer of friendship with God.

3. Reconciliation between humanity and God then flows out into reconciliation among humanity; God's goal and purpose for humanity is to break down every dividing wall of hostility which would frustrate this.

4. It is therefore not possible to separate reconciliation among people from their reconciliation to God; the first flows from the second. Reconciliation among people never stands as a separate activity, or a goal in itself, separate from the reconciliation of humanity to God. It might function as a sign pointing to reconciliation to God, but in the New Testament it always follows and never precedes it. (Matthew 5:24 is not an exception to this; reconciliation with the "brother" is prompted by the prospect of reconciliation with God in the sacrifice to be offered.)

5. Paradoxically, because the reconciled unity of humanity is always connected with God and his purposes, God's offer of peace can actually be a cause of division – division between those who accept God's agenda for reconciliation, and those who reject it, either in relation to its terms or in relation to its goal.

These dynamics shed light on particular examples of conflict and its resolution elsewhere in the New Testament. A key example is the difference between those teaching that Gentiles must be circumcised, and Paul and Barnabas (joined by Peter) opposing them in Acts 15. The division on the issue was sharp and significant: there was "no small dissension and debate" (Acts 15:2; ESV). The process is instructive – after "much debate", they listen to the key testimonies of Peter, Barnabas, and Paul, and then James proposes a way forward with reference to what God has said in Scripture (albeit quoting the Septuagint rather than Hebrew text). And, as Richard Bauckham has demonstrated, the only requirements that are imposed on Gentiles joining the community of believers express a fourfold summary of the Holiness Code from Leviticus 17–26.[18] Because reconciliation is something that God effects (rather than being simply a desirable state of affairs) and because reconciliation between people cannot be separated from reconciliation to God, then the will of God has to be central to the task of reconciliation between parties who are in conflict. For this reason, the intention of God as expressed in the Scriptures is the key reference point in resolving the conflict and effecting reconciliation; it is not merely a case of wise reflection, skill in peacemaking, or the ability to enable people to "disagree well".

Paul's perspective on this issue in his letter to the Galatians illustrates the same dynamic of unity and division highlighted by Joel Green's comment on Luke 15. The reason why Paul sounds so polemical – antagonistic, even – is because he sees God's inclusive invitation as under threat from those who would reject it by imposing additional requirements. If Paul were to act as a simple intermediary, negotiating a middle way between two different viewpoints – his own view and that of his opponents – then this would separate the process of reconciliation from the work of God in Christ. Instead, Paul keeps God's intention to welcome all who turn to him as the touchstone in the dispute; the resolution of difference must be done only in reference to this.

We see the same dynamic at work from another perspective, that of James himself, in his circular letter. Since God is one, in whom there is no changing or turning (James 1:17; 2:19), then there must be unity in every aspect of the lives of believers. We cannot separate faith from action (2:14); we cannot speak with both good and harmful words (3:11); we cannot treat rich and poor in different ways (2:2); and we cannot tolerate conflict and disputes (4:1). Yet, into this vision of unified humanity (which sits most comfortably in the wisdom tradition) James introduces the theme of eschatological judgment and separation (5:1). God will judge those who reject the unity that he is and the unity that he brings.

These observations have profound implications for our approach to current differences in the church, locally, nationally, and globally. On the one hand, it is not possible to argue that the only thing which matters is the truth, and that if other people disagree with us, then they are wrong – and that is just too bad. Jesus' example of restoration and the rebuilding of relations, and Paul's profound concern that the body of Christ be "one", will not allow us off the relational hook so easily. A united new humanity is testimony to the reconciling power of the cross and resurrection.

On the other hand, neither is it possible to argue that reconciliation between warring parties alone should be our aim. Making peace between different groups is no mere human process, and it cannot be achieved by careful listening and mutual understanding, important though these are. Where there are differences of view on matters of theology, pastoral practice, and mission, these cannot be resolved without listening not only to one another, but to what God has done in Christ, and the implications of that as expounded by the apostles in the Scriptures.

Because our reconciliation with one another follows from our reconciliation to God, neither dimension can be neglected nor can they be separated from one another. Reconciliation between people is therefore a necessary part of living out the gospel, but it is not sufficient unless it is attached to and springs from reconciliation to God in the gospel.

***

Questions

1   Have you experienced reconciliation with someone after disagreement
and conflict? What did you learn from it? Has it helped you to disagree
better?

2. What does it mean to be reconciled with God, no longer an enemy but
a friend? How does Jesus secure that reconciliation for us?

3. What does it mean for the church to be entrusted with a "ministry of
reconciliation"? How, in practice, are we to be Christ's ambassadors?

4. Jesus has removed "the dividing wall of hostility" between Christians.
How does this affect our attitude to disagreements within the church?

5. If reconciliation originates in the good news of what God has done
in Christ, to what extent can we be reconciled with others without a
common understanding of the gospel?

3

Division and Discipline in the New Testament Church[1]

Michael B. Thompson

Disagreements between Christians can often lead to separation or schism within the church. New Testament scholar Michael Thompson here examines the key apostolic texts on the subject. He shows how the gospel itself causes division between believers and unbelievers, but that the New Testament warns strongly against those who cause division between Christians. The church is called instead to avoid false teachers and to exercise discipline that leads to repentance, while leaving the ultimate judgment to God.

The gospel brings division

God's purpose in Christ is to bring restoration and unity to his renewed creation. But renewal of life means an inevitable separation from death, just as God's creative word in Genesis 1 led to a division between light and darkness. Love that is not sentimental knows the difference between good and evil, between that which builds up and draws us close to real life and that which tears down and drives us away from God and from each other. When Jesus came bringing good news of God's kingdom, he delighted the humble and those open to his truth, but he also made enemies. Some who were resistant to him and to his message felt threatened by his life-changing power and authority. Although he did not seek to divide people, his mission invariably led some to hostile opposition.

We get our English word "schism" from a Greek noun *schisma* (division) that appears eight times in the New Testament. Twice it refers to the "tear" created in a cloth (Matthew 9:16; Mark 2:21). Three times it occurs in John's Gospel about divisions caused by Jesus. In John 7:43 we read that a crowd of people was divided because of Jesus; some thought he might be a prophet or the Messiah, while others were sure that he was neither; they wanted to arrest him. In John 9:16 some were divided by Jesus' work of healing, on the sabbath, a man blind from birth. And in John 10:19–21 a split arose because of his teachings identifying him closely with God as his Father. In each case, there is no indication that Jesus sought deliberately to divide his hearers; it was the inevitable result of a message which some joyfully accepted but others rejected or simply did not understand.

This helps us to make sense of the saying "I have not come to bring peace but division" (Matthew: "a sword") that appears in Luke 12:51–53 and Matthew 10:34–39.[2] The saying is expounded in the verses that follow, which make it clear that he is speaking about strife within a family and the prospect of one's relatives turning against those who follow Jesus. These verses are not a statement of purpose, as though Christians should seek or effect a separation; they point to the inevitable *result* of family members rejecting the good news and in turn rejecting their loved ones who respond to it.

Again in Acts we read how the gospel message of peace led repeatedly to strong opposition and division. So when Paul and Barnabas preached the good news of Christ in the synagogue at Iconium, many believed but some others became hostile; as a result of their hostility, the residents of Iconium became divided (from the Greek verb *schizo*, the same root as *schisma*; Acts 14:4). Paul and Barnabas sought only peace, but not all people would receive it. Following his Lord's example and teaching, Paul believed in blessing those who persecuted him (Romans 12:14–18) rather than responding to violence with violence. But the good news of Christ does lead at times to division.

Warnings against divisions among Christians

Although the gospel inevitably brings hostility from some who reject it and separates Christians from a way that leads to death (Romans 8:6), those who belong to Christ by faith are part of a family that should never be divided. According to John's Gospel, Jesus prayed that his followers would be one (John 17:11, 22–23). Paul sometimes risked his life for the unity of the body of Christ, most clearly when he carried the financial gift from his churches to their poorer brethren on his last trip to Jerusalem. But from the very beginning there have been temptations and disputes separating Christians from each other.

The remaining three instances of *schisma* in the New Testament are all in Paul's first letter to the Corinthians and reflect the problem of disunity between Christians. At the outset of the letter and in what may well be the epistle's thematic statement, Paul urges his hearers to be in agreement (literally, to "say the same thing") and that there be no divisions (*schismata*) among them (1 Corinthians 1:10). "Saying the same thing" here does not mean uniformity in every matter (what a boring culture that would produce!), but agreement in *aim* or *direction*, in contrast to comparing different leaders and declaring separate loyalties (1 Corinthians 1:12). So Paul goes on to urge them to be united ("knit together") in the same mind and purpose. This is a call to mutual submission to the lordship of Christ, and to each other. Unfortunately, the Corinthians' failure to appreciate the significance of the cross and their proud allegiance to individual leaders were fostering personality cults in the church, undermining their unity in Christ. Paul counters that with a sustained argument in chapters 1–4.

Schisma occurs next in a context emphasizing the importance of the God-given unity and diversity of the church. Some Corinthian Christians were seeking higher status by making much of their spiritual gifts, and in particular, the gift of speaking in tongues. Paul teaches in 1 Corinthians 12:25 that God has composed the body of Christ by giving greater honour to the part that lacked it in order that there should be no *division* (singular) within the body, but the members should have the same concern for one another. There is no room here for attitudes of superiority or inferiority, but rather mutual recognition of one another's importance as indispensable members of Christ.

In 1 Corinthians 11:18 Paul says he has received a report that when they come together as a congregation for worship there are already divisions (*schismata*) among them, and to some extent he believes it. Christians were acting selfishly at the Lord's Supper (at times celebrated as part of a full meal in the early church), with some going hungry and others getting drunk. Rather than building up their oneness in Christ, the occasion was in effect being used for a different purpose – to emphasize the difference between the "haves" and the "have nots". The initial reason Paul gives in 11:19 for believing the report is remarkable: "factions" (the Greek word is *hairesis*, from which we get "heresy") *must* occur among them, so that it will become clear among them who is approved (by God). This difficult statement may reflect Jesus' prophecy of inevitable divisions in Luke 12:51, or possibly an unrecorded saying of Jesus that Justin Martyr cites: "there will be divisions and heresies" (*Dialogue with Trypho* 35.3).

Warnings against those who cause division

Some of the strongest words of condemnation in the New Testament are against those whose actions bring discord and division among God's people (e.g. 1 Corinthians 3:17; 2 Peter 2:1–3). These rebukes make clear the danger of tearing apart the visible body of Christ. They are a warning both to those who innovate at the expense of church unity, with a claim of being "prophetic", and to those who lead others away from the church in response to such innovations.

Sometimes divisions can come from traditionalists who are unable or unwilling to see what God is doing. Paul's pronouncements in Galatians 1:8–9 were aimed at those who insisted that Gentiles had to follow the Old Testament Scriptures in their insistence on circumcision and other Jewish distinctives. His basic concern was that requiring specific ceremonial acts that marked a person out as a Jew ("works of the law") in addition to simple faith in Christ would either exclude Gentile Christians from the body of Christ or put them under a law that was never meant for them. In his strong opposition to excluding others from the kingdom he shared the same perspective as Jesus (Matthew 23:13).

Uninformed Christian zeal or fear can lead to separations God never intends. Some Christians, like the Pharisees, have interpreted the call to holiness (from a root meaning "set apart") as a call to distance themselves deliberately from others. So according to 1 Corinthians 7 some were abstaining from sexual relations within their marriages and considering separating from non-Christian spouses, possibly for the sake of holiness. However, Paul's basic (and sometimes difficult) advice running throughout that chapter is for Christians to remain as they are, maintaining their current responsibilities. Fearing the circumcision party, Peter withdrew from fellowship with Gentiles, which in turn led Barnabas and others to withdraw in hypocrisy (Galatians 2:12–13). But the holiness we see in the example of Jesus was fundamentally positive, not negative. Jesus was not afraid of being near the impure or those with whom he disagreed, but he was profoundly aware that he was set apart *unto* God – he belonged to his heavenly Father and sought to do his will.

Sometimes, however, separation is not simply allowed but required by the New Testament. The critical questions include: from whom?, when?, why? and how? In 2 Corinthians 6:17, for example, Paul quotes Isaiah 52:11 in modified form to call the Corinthians to "come out from them, and be separate from them". But who is he talking about? The passage is difficult, but most likely Paul is warning against participating in pagan cultic meals in Corinth, as he has argued earlier in 1 Corinthians 10:1–22.

Avoiding false teachers

There are a number of New Testament warnings against false teachers and false prophets. Normally these texts call hearers to beware of them or to know them by their fruit (e.g. Matthew 7:15–20; 24:4–26). This is essentially about recognizing them as such, and therefore not being taken in by them.

Jesus' strongest words of criticism in the Gospels are against people who bore great responsibility for spiritual leadership. His blasts at those scribes, Pharisees, and Sadducees who were misleading God's people reflect the seriousness of their error. He saw their corruption as something like yeast in a loaf of bread, spreading and affecting the whole community (Mark 8:15). Matthew emphasizes their *teachings* as yeast (Matthew 16:6–12); Luke points to the hypocrisy of their private behaviour (Luke 12:1–3). Jesus taught the danger of temptations to sin and that drastic action sometimes needed to be taken to minimize the cause of such temptations (Matthew 18:7–9).[3]

Twice in his letters, Paul refers to "false brothers" (2 Corinthians 11:26; Galatians 2:4). Arguably in both cases "false" is referring not to whether they were baptized Christians but to their teachings as mistaken or contrary to the truth in their opposition to Paul and aspects of his gospel of grace. In Galatians they were people who wanted to compel compliance to the Torah in addition to faith in Christ, and this is most likely the case in 2 Corinthians.

Surprisingly, little is said explicitly about separating from false teachers. Even in the case of Paul's warning of "savage wolves" who were to come and those from within the church who would distort the truth, the specific instruction is to keep watch and be alert (Acts 20:28–31). It would be taken for granted that one should keep a healthy distance from wolves, and we should be wary of building a case from silence. The leaders of the church would be expected to refute such teachers. In fact, there are some texts that advocate separation from those who persist in teaching serious error.

ROMANS 16:17–20

Although he has previously urged the "weak" and "strong" to respect each other in their differences in faith, in Romans 16:17–20 Paul addresses something else. He solemnly warns his hearers to take note of those who create dissensions (*dichostasiai*; elsewhere in the New Testament only in Galatians 5:20) and stumbling blocks (*skandala*) contrary to the teaching which the Roman Christians had already received. The Romans should continuously "avoid" such people; the tense and meaning of the verb here connotes "to stay away from" or "to keep steering clear of" them.

We do not know exactly whom Paul is talking about here. He probably does not have specific individuals in mind, since he is writing from Corinth and has never been to Rome before. His language comes from the Old Testament wisdom tradition, but he has already experienced such people in the past (especially in Corinth). From their fruit – the effects of the actions of troublemakers – Paul knows their real motives, because by putting their own agenda above the needs of others they serve not Christ but their own appetites. What they are doing divides the faithful and tempts them to spiritual ruin. Their method is typically plausible speech and fine sounding words which deceive the hearts of the innocent; their end he says is evil, aligned with the Adversary. But the God of peace will one day put an end to that Adversary (Romans 16:20).

2 PETER 2:1–22

The entire second chapter of 2 Peter is an extended warning against false teachers that makes for sober reading. Many scholars consider the detailed description to apply to contemporaries of the biblical author, although it reads as a prophecy that sadly continues to be fulfilled in history. In contrast to the itinerant intruders in Jude, these false teachers appear to be members of the churches who introduce notions rooted in their culture that are contrary to the gospel. Their opinions (*haireseis*) result in destruction and are so serious as to amount to a denial of Christ – probably either by denying his future return or by their immorality.

The error begins with scepticism and a denial of the divine authority of the Old Testament and of the return of Christ (1:20–21; 2:10; 3:3–10). This in turn contributes to profound ethical failure, since there is no ultimate accountability. Subject to greed and arrogant in confidently denying the power of the devil and his angels, the false teachers are slaves to drunkenness and to their own sexual desires. With deceptive, persuasive rhetoric they entice and mislead the unstable with promises of illusory freedom, despise any authority that would correct them, and bring disrepute to the Christian faith. They are so compromised by readopting non-Christian values that holiness cannot be seen (2:20–21).

Rather than calling for their excommunication, 2 Peter's response is that they will surely not escape God's judgment. They may be supremely confident, but they are on the path to destruction. Their appearance among the faithful is inevitable. Nevertheless, the readers have been forewarned and need to be vigilant not to be led away by their error; the best antidote is stability resulting from paying attention to what has been received, and growing in grace and the knowledge of Christ (1:5–15; 3:17–18).

JUDE 3–19
Jude's warnings against false teachers are very similar to those in 2 Peter, although the opponents appear to be itinerants who come from outside the community. His readers are to "struggle/contend" for the faith because these antinomians are turning the grace of God into licentiousness and denying Christ (verses 3–4). Characterized by immorality, they are dreamers (perhaps referring to claimed visionary experiences) who reject authority, ridicule angelic powers, and selfishly feed themselves at Christian love-feasts (meals which included the eucharist). They grumble, boast, and flatter, and their

sensuality causes divisions, reflecting their lack of the Spirit (verses 16 and 19). Their coming has been prophesied and they will surely suffer judgment from God (verses 14–18).

Rather than calling explicitly for separation from these false teachers, Jude like 2 Peter emphasizes their judgment to come. Nevertheless, even with such strong warnings there is a note of hope for those in danger. Jude 22–23 urges the hearers to have mercy on those who doubt (or possibly, who "dispute"), to save others by snatching them from the fire (persuading those who will listen to turn from their error), and to have mercy (in the fear of God) on others, "hating even the tunic soiled by their flesh". This last phrase is a vivid metaphor warning against spiritual contamination using the imagery of a garment soiled with excrement. The last group may be spiritually "filthy" and headed for ruin, but that does not exempt the church from a redemptive responsibility toward them.

2 JOHN 10–11

These verses prohibit hearers from continuing (indicated by the Greek tense) to welcome and to greet any person who does not bring "this teaching" (verse 10). The reason given for the lack of hospitality appears in the following verse: one who greets such a person shares in that person's evil deeds. In context "this teaching" refers to the "teaching of Christ", specifically the doctrine of the incarnation (verses 7 and 9; compare 1 John 4:1–3). Second John strongly warns against any such "progressive" thinker who "goes ahead" (*proagein*) and denies Christianity's fundamental tenet: that the Messiah has come in the flesh. The greeting would have involved more than saying "Hello"; Christian hospitality normally included provisions for further journey (3 John 6, 8). But "greeting" heretics in this way would be to provide them with support and material resources to spread their errors even further.

The error of misunderstanding or misusing such a severe separation warning is reflected in 3 John. If welcoming heretics was a danger, Diotrephes' inflated sense of self-importance led him to an opposite extreme. He denied apostolic authority, refused to welcome Christians, prevented others from welcoming them, and even put those who were hospitable out of the church (3 John 9–10).

In summary, the New Testament strongly warns against those who deny essential Christian teachings (such as the incarnation), indulge their own appetites, and so bring divisions among the people of God. A repeated theme is that caving in to one's own desires carries with it the cost of one's ability to tell truth from error. The church is told to avoid such people. The threat of their coming judgment, however, does not change the fact that they are human beings in need of redemption, people for whom Christ died.

Judging others

The fundamental teaching concerning people who tear the church apart is that *they will be judged by God*. Over and over again, the followers of Jesus are told that those who mislead or divide his people will ultimately have to answer for it. The New Testament frequently appeals to the fact of the final judgment in order to commend right behaviour, although this theme is often neglected today.

Jesus was acutely aware that some of his followers would be tempted to take the matter of judgment into their own hands, and he warned them on several occasions against it. The parable of the wheat and the tares/weeds (Matthew 13:24–30, 36–43) highlights the mixture of good and evil in the world and the danger of uprooting the wheat when people seek to remove the weeds. The point is that separation is not ours to instigate, but it will surely come (see Matthew 13:47–50). Christ is the one who will ultimately do the separating, and he can be trusted to do so on the last day. Impatience too easily leads us to take that matter into our own hands.

It is of course true that "by their fruits you shall know them"; the difficulty is when to measure the fruits. Thankfully, the parable of the prodigal son does not stop with his experience in the far country. God alone knows the state of hearts; our responsibility is not to prejudge people's destinies, but to seek to encourage everyone to move forward in faith – wherever they may be spiritually on a given day. Within the church this means treating people with the "charitable assumption" that their profession to belong to Christ is true and encouraging them to live by it.

To quote Jesus' warning against judging others lest we be judged (Matthew 7:1–2; Luke 6:37) as an argument against any form of church discipline, however, fails to see that Jesus and his followers themselves exercised appropriate judgment and took difficult decisions with people. The teaching here most likely contrasts the practice of those Pharisees who so often passed hypocritical judgment on the behaviour of others. The target is not critical thinking *per se*, but a self-centred sense of superiority that regards others without due consideration of one's own sinfulness (Romans 2:1) and without mercy and compassion.

It is one thing to be characteristically negative about others who fall short of our own standards; it is another to offer a word of correction in the same spirit that led Jesus to rebuke serious errors. To fail to help people to repent when their actions are destroying others and the unity God has built among his people, shows much less grace than a word of correction offered in humble awareness of our own weakness and failings. The temptation for Christians to prejudge other Christians strikes those on *both* sides of any division; those who quickly quote "Judge not…" to deflect criticism are sometimes in the very process of doing what they would prohibit.

Church discipline

Alongside warnings against schismatics and false prophets, the New Testament teaches the need for appropriate discipline within the church. We should read these texts against the background of ancient Judaism, which sometimes demanded far more severe penalties. Deuteronomy, for example, repeatedly calls for the death of offenders in order to purge the sin. In the first century, people at the synagogue could be whipped, as was Paul on several occasions (2 Corinthians 11:24). Rabbinic practice (difficult to date with certainty) included placing a ban on the offender for a minimum of thirty days if he were a religious leader. Later practice limited the ban to a maximum of thirty days, renewable for a further thirty days if the person failed to repent. If that failed, a more severe separation was imposed. At Qumran, troublesome members were sometimes temporarily or permanently excluded from the community (1QS 6.24–7.25; CD 9.23; 20.3). Six texts from the New Testament are particularly relevant to the practice of early Christian discipline.

MATTHEW 18:15–18

This is the clearest passage in the Gospels on the subject of discipline; its focus is forgiveness and its goal is restitution. Matthew's text addresses the question of one person's sin against another rather than a sin against the community, but the principle of accountability in love established here came to be applied later in the church towards a wider range of situations. The proper Christian response to personal offence from another Christian is to pursue reconciliation by leading the wrongdoer to acknowledge and turn back from the sin. In this way we imitate the shepherd of 18:10–14 who goes after the stray sheep. Here the offence in mind must be serious and intentional, since love is patient and "covers" a multitude of sins (1 Peter 4:8).

What is often missed is that the call to point out the fault in Matthew 18:15 (literally "reprove him" or "convict him"; Luke 17:3 has "rebuke him") has its roots in Leviticus 19:17: "You shall not hate in your heart anyone of your kin; you shall reprove your neighbour, or you will incur guilt yourself," which is immediately followed in Leviticus by the commandment to love one's neighbour as one's self. Real love loves enough to confront serious sin rather than to pretend it does not exist. The goal of the confrontation is not retributive, but to expose guilt in such a way that the person is persuaded of his or her sin and their wayward direction is changed.

The sister or brother who hears and accepts the word of correction has been regained.

If confrontation in private does not suffice, one does not give up on the offender. The second stage of pursuit is to bring one or two others to witness a further attempt to persuade the wrongdoer (Matthew 18:16). The purpose of the extra witnesses (echoing the principle in Deuteronomy 19:15; continued in 2 Corinthians 13:1 and 1 Timothy 5:19) is not simply legal to ensure against false accusation; their presence reflects the seriousness of the situation, but the goal remains repentance and restoration. If a third stage is necessary, the matter is brought before the congregation (the *ekklesia*; Matthew 18:17) to support a final attempt to convince and reconcile the erring disciple.

If that fails, the offender is to be shunned by the community even as unrepentant, notorious tax collectors and Gentiles were socially excluded as outsiders in Jewish society. Practically, this would include the community at least keeping their distance, not sharing meals, and certainly not allowing them to join in their most sacred services of worship. It is effectively excommunication. It would be contrary to the spirit of the entire passage and the rest of Jesus' teaching if the goal of such exclusion were punitive. The purpose, even in the exclusion, is to shock the wrongdoer into eventual repentance by making them realize the gravity of their failure to repent. The goal is to win them back, which may well be the aim of the prayers mentioned in Matthew 18:19. The basic principle of at least two warnings before a penalty is apparently unparalleled in ancient Judaism, apart from in Titus 3:10–11 (see below).

1 CORINTHIANS 5

This passage is the most detailed and specific case of discipline in the New Testament epistles; a man was apparently engaged in an ongoing incestuous relationship with his stepmother. Paul was more shocked by the Corinthian church's response to flagrant immorality than he was by the offender's failure. Well aware of human weakness, he was not surprised when people erred. It was another thing, however, for that failure to be as notorious as incest (condemned in Leviticus 18:8 and Deuteronomy 22:30, and repugnant even in Graeco-Roman culture) and for it to continue (indicated by the Greek tense) uncorrected and even celebrated by the church.

The church's proper response should have been to mourn. They should have mourned for their sinful brother's failure, lack of repentance, and prospect of judgment (see 2 Corinthians 12:21), but also for the shame brought upon the community and perhaps in repentance for their corporate implication in his failure. A response of mourning would have driven out the man from among them if their grief and admonition did not bring him to his senses. Instead, they were puffed up with arrogance and even proud of their tolerance (5:2, 6). Whether they were intimidated by the man's own wealth and influence is uncertain, but clearly they thought themselves to be wise, spiritually enlightened, and progressive. They were in grave danger.

Paul responds decisively. In this case of incest he does not need to hear more about the circumstances or mitigating factors such as how "fulfilling" the relationship might be. He has already made a judgment, and solemnly declares that the offender is to be "handed over to Satan for the destruction of the flesh" (5:5). His language is strange to us, but most likely refers to excommunication. He is not talking about physical death, as in the case of Ananias and Sapphira (Acts 5), but expulsion from the security of Christ's visible body back into the kingdom of this world dominated by the Adversary. The man is to be "removed" or "purged", driven out from Christian fellowship and worship (5:13, using a stronger form of the Greek root used in 5:2). They are not to associate with him or even eat with him (5:11).

This is not an act of vindictiveness, but of compassion, because the aim is the man's salvation (5:5; compare Paul's pastoral concern in the case of 2 Corinthians 2:3–10). The "destruction of the flesh" probably refers either to putting to death – in repentance – one's own way of life that disobeys God (Colossians 3:5; "crucifying the flesh",

Galatians 5:24) or suffering enough of separation from the life-giving experience of the Spirit once enjoyed in Christian fellowship to bring the man back to God. In any case, a physical expulsion is called for in order to bring about a spiritual redemption for him.

But discipline is not simply for the individual; it protects the church. The Corinthians are acting as though tolerating the spiritual cancer of sin is a healthy thing, when in fact like leaven it spreads, affecting the whole (5:6). Using imagery from Passover bread, Paul calls for the leaven to be "cleaned out", so that the church may be a new loaf – unleavened as they already are in Christ (5:7). There is no room for wickedness, nor for malice in response to it; the need is for sincerity *and* truth (5:8).

Paul could have stopped here, but he does not want his hearers to misunderstand what he means. An earlier letter (which we do not have) had warned them not to associate with (*sunanamignusthai*, "to mix with") sexually immoral people (5:9). Some must have understood him to be referring to non-Christians, which would have the effect of isolating the church, especially given Corinth's reputation for sexual licence. Paul clarifies that he is talking about any professing Christian whose lifestyle is characterized by immorality – or for that matter idolatry, coveting, extortion, slandering, drunkenness, or robbery (5:10–11). Instead of judging outsiders and distancing themselves from people who need to hear the good news of Christ, the community should keep its distance from individuals who claim to believe, yet whose lives bring the transforming grace of the gospel into disrepute. The quotation calling for purging the evildoer comes from Deuteronomy, which originally called for death. For Paul, separation from life in Christ's body was just as serious.

2 THESSALONIANS 3:6–15

In context this strong command ("in the name of our Lord Jesus Christ") called for the readers to keep some distance (*stellein*, "to avoid", "to keep away") from idlers who sponged off the community and refused to work when they were able. Whether their idleness was influenced by the kind of eschatological expectation corrected in the previous chapter (2:1–2) is disputed, but clearly they were using their leisure to meddle (3:11). In his first letter Paul had urged the congregation to admonish such people (1 Thessalonians 5:14), and the distance called for in 2 Thessalonians appears to be a further step in correction since they are continuing to choose to live contrary to the teaching they have received. Aware that the idlers' poor example could spread, Paul wants his readers to follow the apostolic example of self-support and not grow weary of doing good (3:7–10, 13). He is probably also concerned here about the bad name such behaviour could give the church among their neighbours.

Apparently exclusion is envisaged from meals at least (3:10). However, the language does not go so far as to imply full excommunication. If the idle person (or anyone) refuses to obey Paul's admonitions, however, his exhortation in 3:14–15 takes correction a step further. The community is to "take note" (the verb can mean "to note in writing") of the person and to stop associating with them. The latter verb (*sunanamignusthai*) is the same word he uses in 1 Corinthians 5:9, 11. It would include at least exclusion from the Lord's Supper, with the purpose of shaming the offender. In this instance, the person is not denying the central tenets of the gospel or living in flagrant sexual immorality, but nevertheless is unwilling to repent of a lifestyle that is unfaithful to the rest of the community. Paul's addition in verse 15 makes it clear that discipline is not to be administered with hostility; the errant person is not an enemy but remains a member of the family (literally "a brother"). Repentance and restoration is the goal.

1 TIMOTHY 1:19–20

Emphasizing the importance of keeping a clear conscience, the apostle here contrasts the success he wishes for Timothy with the failure experienced by two men who had professed to be Christians but who went on to make a shipwreck of their faith. He does not say here how they did so, although they may well be the coppersmith

Alexander of 2 Timothy 4:14–15 (who did Paul great harm, strongly opposing his message) and Hymenaeus of 2 Timothy 2:17–18 (who denied the future resurrection and overturned the faith of some). He does not reflect here on the length or stages of discipline in their cases but rather on the outcome.

The language of "handing" them "over to Satan" is best interpreted in the light of 1 Corinthians 5:5 where the same Greek terms are used. They were excommunicated, expelled from Christian fellowship back into the world dominated by the Adversary. No doubt part of the purpose was to protect the church, which had been damaged by their teachings, but the stated purpose here is redemptive: so that they might be *taught* (*paideuesthai*, often used of discipline) to stop blaspheming in their teachings – and presumably, to repent.

1 TIMOTHY 5:20

This call to rebuke (*elenchein*) those who persist in sin follows a warning against accepting accusations against an elder unless there are two or three witnesses, and so has *serious* error in view. What is unusual here is the addition that the rebuke should be made in the presence of all members of the church (reflecting an advanced stage of correction) and the purpose – that the rest (of the elders? of the church?) literally "may have fear". This last phrase probably refers to the fear of God, in contrast to the bold arrogance involved in publicly rejecting the tradition received.

TITUS 3:10–11

Here we find some similarity with the disciplinary process taught in Matthew 18:15–18. The problem is a "factious" (*hairetikos*) person – that is, someone whose stubborn promotion of sectarian opinions keeps causing divisions; the response is admonition (*nouthesia*, a word connoting pastoral concern). The context indicates that controversies over the Old Testament Law may be specifically in mind (3:9). After two warnings (the use of "first" and "second" may hint at separate stages with different circumstances), Titus should "have nothing more to do with" such a person. The verb here (*paraiteisthai*) means "to reject" or "to repudiate" (1 Timothy 5:11; Hebrews 12:25), suggesting excommunication. Such serious discipline is justified because the factious person is demonstrating himself to be perverse, continuing in sin as one who is self-condemned. As elsewhere, the sin is not the mistaken opinions that are held (however sincerely), but the damaging division of the congregation that results from the individual pressing forward with dubious teachings. That destructive effect leads to the need for discipline.

Conclusion

Although his message and example was one of love, peace, redemption, and forgiveness, Jesus himself caused an inevitable division between believers and unbelievers. The gospel message still divides today. But the New Testament warns strongly against those who, one way or another, divide the body of Christ. False teachers in particular lead people into serious error, away from the true liberation of following Jesus; they can be known by their fruits. The church is told to avoid them, and, if necessary, to drive the unrepentant away. It is worth noting, however, that every case of discipline in the New Testament concerns the failings of *individuals* who profess the faith – there are no examples of the apostles excluding entire congregations.

Biblical discipline is not punitive, but excludes in order to protect and aims to restore. The practice of gracious and effective discipline of this kind, in the spirit in which Jesus called for it, is not often seen in the church today. The risk of acting in anger rather than with love is great. Equally dangerous, however, is to allow spiritual cancer to spread instead of confronting a threat to the entire community.

As has been seen, a recurring theme in the New Testament is that of leaving the ultimate judgment to God. This does not absolve us of obligation to exercise collective spiritual discernment, and hence church discipline, when the unity of the community is at risk. But it should caution us against acting impulsively or precipitately. The seven churches in Revelation 2–3 are rebuked for serious error and called to repentance, but are not told to dissociate from each other, and Christians are not instructed to separate from them. Rather it is Jesus Christ who will discipline (Revelation 2:5, 16, 22; 3:3, 16). In the meantime, Paul's instructions to the Romans are essential guidance for all churches faced by disagreements, disputes, and divisions:

> *Bless those who persecute you; bless and do not curse them... Live in harmony with one another; do not be haughty, but associate with the lowly; do not claim to be wiser than you are... Why do you pass judgment on your brother or sister? Or you, why do you despise your brother or sister? For we will all stand before the judgment seat of God. For it is written, "As I live, says the Lord, every knee shall bow to me, and every tongue shall give praise to God." So then, each of us will be accountable to God... May the God of steadfastness and encouragement grant you to live in harmony with one another, in accordance with Christ Jesus, so that together you may with one voice glorify the God and Father of our Lord Jesus Christ. (Romans 12:14, 16; 14:10–12; 15:5–6; NRSV)*

***

Questions

1. What are your experiences of division or separation within the church? What lessons have you learned from them?

2. Why does the New Testament warn so strongly against division and those who cause it?

3. In the light of New Testament teaching, how do we identify and respond

to false teachers in the church? What needs to change in the way we practise church discipline today?

4. When is it right for us to judge? What does it mean in practice to leave judgment to God?

5. Is "good disagreement" compatible with division or discipline?

4
Pastoral Theology for Perplexing Topics: Paul and *Adiaphora*
Tom Wright

The apostle Paul was passionate for both the unity and holiness of the church, and held these priorities together as he applied pastoral wisdom to areas of major disagreement. Through an exploration of key New Testament texts, Tom Wright presents Paul's vision of the church as the new covenant and new creation people. He shows how this vision helped Paul in his day, and can help us in ours, to distinguish between differences which don't matter (*adiaphora*) and differences which do matter.

Introduction

Anyone reading swiftly through Paul's letters looking for regularly recurring themes can hardly miss his constant insistence on the unity of the church. Believing Jews and believing Gentiles are to worship together, learning to set aside differences of diet and holy days (Romans 14–15). They are to eat together, celebrating their shared membership in Abraham's family in which there is neither Jew nor Greek, slave nor free, no "male and female" (Galatians 2–4). Together they form the holy temple where the living God dwells through his Spirit (Ephesians 2), and the varied ministries they are given are to serve this unity and the church's resulting growth to maturity (Ephesians 4). Threats from opponents are not to destroy this unity (Philippians 1:27–28); differences of background, ethnic origin, and culture are to count for nothing (Colossians 3); mutual love must bind the disparate membership together (1 Thessalonians 4); the greatest social division of the ancient world (that between master and slave) was to be overcome by the power of shared family life in the Messiah (Philemon). Towering over even these strong passages we find the truly extraordinary exhortation of Philippians 2:2–5: "bring your thinking into line with one another... hold on to the same love, bring your innermost lives into harmony, fix your minds on the same object... Look after each other's best interests, not your own." How are they to do this? Nothing less than the self-abnegating mind of the Messiah himself must be their model (2:6–11).

Above even this, however, we have 1 Corinthians. In this letter, unity is a main theme from one angle after another. Personality cults must not pull the church apart: that would be to destroy the temple of God (chapters 1–3). Believers must not take one another to court (chapter 6). Christians who live in a pagan environment (that is, more or less all Paul's churches) are to learn how to navigate the tricky moral challenges of that culture with the paramount task being to remain in fellowship with one another (chapters 8–10). There are to be no divisions at the Lord's table (chapter 11): this may indicate the threatening presence of a rich/poor division in the church, but it may go wider as well. The three great chapters 12, 13, and 14 come at the task of unity from numerous angles. There are varieties of gifts, ministries, and operations, but a single Spirit, Lord, and God, and this means that there is one differentiated body of the Messiah, each member of which must respect all the others (chapter 12). When the church meets for worship, all that is done must promote unity and upbuilding (chapter 14). In between these two there is the incomparable poem on love (chapter 13). The long chapter on resurrection (chapter 15) does not contribute overtly to the theme of unity, but a close study of the whole letter indicates that belief in resurrection lies underneath most of the preceding arguments. Thus Paul's letters in general, and 1 Corinthians in particular, insist on a unity in the church which transcends issues of ethnicity, social status, and different vocations.

To the modern Western mind, all this might speak of a "tolerance" in which the imperative of unity would push onto the back burner all questions of actual behaviour. Never mind our differences of behaviour; let's simply enjoy fellowship with one another! This might, indeed, seem to be the natural corollary of what Paul says about different views on dietary laws and observance of holy days in Romans 14; and such a conclusion might seem to be reinforced by the doctrine that claims central place in many accounts of Paul's thought, namely justification by faith apart from works of the law. Indeed, Romans 14 might with good reason be seen as the direct outworking of justification: "justification by faith" in Romans 3 and 4 leads to "fellowship by faith" in Romans 14 and 15. The shared faith in Jesus as Messiah, and in the fulfilment of the divine purpose through him, overcomes all cultural and ideological differences. Unity is what matters: never mind the varieties of practice.

And yet. Our quick cursory reading indicates just as obviously that this was not how Paul saw things. Romans itself is full of "ethical" instruction, both in the broad general level of chapters 6 and 8 (where the defeat of the "power" called "sin" means that believers are set free and must not re-submit), and in the specifics of chapters 12 and 13 – and also in the way in which, through the logic of the letter as a whole, the catalogue of vicious and dehumanizing behaviour in chapters 1 and 2 is reversed, first in the character of Abraham in chapter 4, then in the life of the Spirit in chapter 8, and then in the "renewal of the mind" – and of the behaviour which results – in chapter 12. The lists, in Galatians 5, of "the works of the flesh" and "the fruit of the Spirit" are framed with a dire warning: those who do the former "will not inherit God's kingdom" (a phrase echoed elsewhere too), while those who do the latter "have crucified the flesh with its passions and desires". Ephesians 4 gives a solemn warning against living in the way ordinary pagans do, going into considerable detail about the styles of behaviour in question.

Philippians 3:17–19 gives a tearful warning about those "whose end is destruction, whose god is the belly, who set their minds on earthly things"; the latter phrase is picked up in Colossians 3 in the larger instruction to set the mind on things above. First Thessalonians 4 issues clear commandments about the way in which Christian behaviour is not to reflect the pagan world around. Finally, returning to 1 Corinthians, we find clear, strong, and detailed instruction both about what to do when people in the church behave as though they are still pagans – or worse than pagans! (chapters 5–6) – and how to avoid pagan-style behaviour creeping into the church in the first place (chapter 10). Clearly, if Paul is keen on unity, he is equally keen on holiness.

Is he thereby being inconsistent? Some might think so. Some might suppose that his sharp moral judgments are simply the hangover from his former culture, not least the moral scruples that he had had as a zealous Pharisee. Some would go further, and insist that if "justification by faith not law" meant what it said then the whole idea of "rules", of whatever sort, should be outlawed in a truly Pauline theology. If we believe in grace rather than law, so one hears it said, the kind of definite and specific moral judgments we find in Galatians 5, Colossians 3, or 1 Corinthians 5 and 6 should ultimately have no place.

One kind of answer to this is the theological and philosophical argument we find in a book like Miroslav Volf's *Exclusion and Embrace* (1996). It isn't enough to say "embrace" (that is, "include"); there is such a thing as real evil, and if we fail to name it and shame it we are merely incorporating radical dehumanization into the ongoing life of the community. The scandals that have come to light recently in many walks of life show well enough what that dehumanization looks like: in the brave new world of the 1960s and beyond, many treated older moral codes as out of date and irrelevant. As usual, many in the churches went along for the ride, whether in practice or whether, sometimes using apparently Pauline language, in theological theory. The work of Volf and others has shown this up as thoroughly inadequate, the more powerfully in Volf's case because of his own experience in facing, as a Croatian, the question "How can I love my Serbian neighbour?" Answer: only through the initial "exclusion" in which evil is recognized for what it is – and which itself always aims at an ultimate, and hard-won, "embrace". That kind of theoretical discussion needs to continue.

The present chapter, however, comes at the same questions from the angle of Pauline exegesis. Paul, I shall argue, is not at all inconsistent in his double stress on unity and holiness. Both are functions of his deepest theological insights; both are to be attained through the practical inhabiting of those insights, through their incorporation into the DNA of the Messiah's community and of every Spirit-indwelt believer. Properly understood, they do not form a paradox, pulling in opposite directions. They actually reinforce one another.

To understand this, we need to grasp the heart of Paul's vision of the church. That will be my first main section below. To apply it, in my second main section, we need to understand how Paul sees the question of *adiaphora*, "things indifferent": how do we know which things are "indifferent" and which are not? How do we tell the difference between the differences which make a difference (for Paul, certain differences of behaviour and lifestyle) and the differences which don't make a difference (for Paul, certain other differences which might equally be seen as "behaviour" and "lifestyle")? For Paul, it seems, our modern generalized terms "behaviour" and "lifestyle" do not take us to the heart of it! We have to be more specific.

This is where the research of recent generations really helps. A great deal of careful work has been done to locate Paul and his communities within their social and cultural worlds, and to understand how Paul's vision of the church played out in those complex spheres of existence. I am implicitly drawing on this research in what follows.

Paul's vision of the church

Every Pauline letter makes its own distinctive contribution to our full understanding of Paul's vision of the church. But it is 1 Corinthians, where the puzzle I have identified finds clearest expression, that arguably offers the richest portrait of his ecclesiology, meshing with strands of thought deployed elsewhere and holding them together within a rich harmony. In 1 Corinthians 10, Paul describes the church as a new kind of people, neither Jewish nor pagan: be blameless, he says, before Jews, before Greeks, and before God's church. This fits with the tripartite division that emerges in chapter 1 in people's varied reactions to the gospel: Jews demand signs, Greeks seek wisdom, but we proclaim the crucified Messiah. The gospel is folly to Greeks, scandalous to Jews, but for us who are being saved – a third category! – it is God's wisdom and power.

Something new has happened in the world with the Messiah's death and resurrection and with the sending of the Spirit. For Paul, this is a new sort of humanity – indeed, a "new creation", as in Galatians 6 or 2 Corinthians 5. In 1 Corinthians 15 and Romans 5–8 it is clear that this "new creation" is the new thing for which the original creation was made in the first place. In the new creation, the original Adamic purpose and destiny is at last fulfilled. But this radical newness does not simply sweep off the board all the signs of divine purpose in the long years of Israelite and Jewish scriptural narrative. At the start of 1 Corinthians 10, Paul identifies the church as the true descendants of the Exodus generation, and thereby *narrates the Jew-plus-Gentile church into the longer story of Israel.* "Our ancestors", he says, "were all baptized into Moses": they were rescued from Egypt, yet with many of them God was not pleased. The force of the ethical warning is missed unless the premise is grasped: those who are now "in the Messiah" can and must understand themselves as the new representatives of the single great narrative in which the Exodus from Egypt was part of the foundation.

Exegetes today struggle to say this accurately and without the appearance of anti-Jewish feeling. Despite the phraseology that used to be employed, Paul never says either "new Israel" or "true Israel"; yet he repeatedly implies something like that, not least in 1 Corinthians 10 itself when he compares the church to "Israel according to the flesh" (10:16). His description of "the Jew" in Romans 2:25–29, and of "the circumcision" in Philippians 3:2–11, indicates well enough what he is doing. He is casting those "in the Messiah", Jew and Greek together, as the single family in which the great promises to Israel will be fulfilled, promises that through them the ancient curse of sin and death will be undone and the creator's purposes for the world will be accomplished at last.

One way to get this clear – perhaps the best, or even the only way – is to insist that for Paul *Jesus the Messiah is Israel in person*. God has done for him, in raising him from the dead, what Paul as a Pharisee had supposed God would do for all Israel at the end. He is thereby constituted as Israel's representative. It is not the case, in other words, that Paul thinks in terms of God exchanging a Jewish family for a non-Jewish one (the classic "supersession" position). Rather, if Jesus is Israel's Messiah then Israel is identified as the people who are now grouped around him. That, after all, was how first-century Jewish thinking would work; there were many would-be messianic movements within a century or so either side of Jesus, and any claim that so-and-so was the Messiah was *ipso facto* a claim that God's people were now to be seen in terms of their allegiance to this figure. Did Paul think that Jesus was the Messiah? Of course. Did recognizing someone as Messiah imply that God's people were regrouped around him? Naturally. Was that a non-Jewish or even anti-Jewish thing to suggest? Of course not.

The point, anyway, is that for Paul the Messiah's people are *both* a "new creation" *and* the fulfilment of the divine intention for Israel. This chimes with the insistence in Romans 4 and Galatians 3 and 4 that the single messianic family is the true family promised to Abraham in the first place. This family – here is the famous doctrine – is "justified by faith", since this "faith", which Paul defines as the belief that God raised Jesus from the dead, and the confession that he is *kyrios*, Lord, is the one and only defining mark that the family bears. The resurrection indicates that Jesus' death was indeed "for our sins" (Galatians 1:4), and part of the meaning of that is that "Gentile sinners" (Galatians 2:15) are "sinners" no more, and can therefore be full members of the family, whose other members – believing Jews – have themselves "died to the law through the law, that [they] might live to God" (Galatians 2:19).

The point of all this for our larger discussion may not be immediately apparent, but it can be drawn out easily in two points. (a) The divine intention, as Paul saw it unveiled in the messianic events concerning Jesus, was to create a single worldwide family; *and therefore any practices that functioned as symbols dividing different ethnic groups could not be maintained as absolutes within this single family.* Thus the major marks of Israel's ethnic distinctiveness – circumcision, food laws, sabbath, and the Jerusalem Temple itself – were to be set aside, not because they were bad, not given by God, or representative of a shabby or second-rate kind of "religion", but because of "messianic eschatology", the fact that in Jesus Israel's God had done at last the new thing he had always promised. (b) This divine intention, glimpsed in Scriptures upon which Paul drew, and sketched out in much of his teaching, was that this single family would, by the Spirit's work, embody, represent, and carry forward the plan of "new creation", the plan which had been the intention for Israel from the beginning; *and that therefore any practices that belonged to the dehumanizing, anti-creation world of sin and death could likewise not be maintained within this new-creation family.* The first principle explains why certain things are now "indifferent"; the second, why certain other things are not. This is the difference between the two kinds of "difference". We note that in this double-edged ecclesiology Jewish believers are required to give up the absolutizing of their specific ethnic boundary markers, and erstwhile pagan believers are required to give up elements of their former life which they have taken for granted. This doesn't mean that Jews are being paganized (though Jewish apologists have frequently charged the church with that, sometimes with good reason), and it doesn't mean that pagans are Judaizing (though from very early on some were tempted to do just that). It means that both are summoned to belong to the family of the crucified and risen Messiah.

This distinction between (a) the differences which don't make a difference, and which one must therefore "tolerate", and (b) those which do make a difference, and which one must therefore not tolerate, is thus rooted in the twin theological poles around which Paul's thought revolves: creation and new creation on the one hand; covenant and new covenant on the other. In both, there is appropriate continuity and discontinuity, provided repeatedly by the model of cross and resurrection. The old is judged on the cross; the resurrection, ushering in the new, nevertheless is the true retrieval of the created goodness of the old. Without the cross, and its judgment, we are not taking seriously the fact of sin and death. In Volf's terms, we are trying to get "embrace" without "exclusion". Without the resurrection, as the transformative re-enlivening of the condemned creation, we have all exclusion and no embrace. In terms of creation and new creation, the new creation retrieves and fulfils the intention for the original creation, in which the coming together of heaven and earth is reflected in the coming together of male and female. This vision of the original creative purpose was retained by Israel, the covenant people, the "bride" of YHWH, and the strong sexual ethic which resulted formed one noticeable mark of distinction between the Jewish people and the wider world. This was highlighted dramatically in the Torah with the contrast between Judah's "pagan" behaviour in Genesis 38 and Joseph's rejection of Potiphar's wife's advances in Genesis 39.

Within the Jewish world this sexual ethic was seen as the direct outflow of creational monotheism: the One God had created the world, including the complementary and fruit-bearing differentiation in the animal kingdom. It wasn't just that sexual malpractice happened to take place, often enough, in the precincts of pagan temples. There was an organic connection. If you worship idols, your image-bearing capacity diminishes, and you fail to carry forward the creative purposes of God. That is why, to look at the positive side, when Abraham believes in God's creative and life-giving power, in Romans 4, the corruption of Romans 1 is reversed and he and Sarah conceive a child in their old age. The paradox then becomes clear: *Paul insists that the markers which distinguish Jew from Gentile are no longer relevant in the new, messianic dispensation; but the Jewish-style worship of the One God, and the human male/female life which reflects that creational monotheism, is radically reinforced.*

Paul is clear, though many interpreters have not been, how this works out. Circumcision and uncircumcision are nothing; what matters is new creation. Food will not commend us to God; whether we eat or refuse to eat, we glorify God. Keeping this or that holy day, or not keeping them, is not a barrier to fellowship with others who do it differently. In the Messiah, and in the renewed Abrahamic family which is called into being through his death-for-sins and his new-creational resurrection, there is neither Jew nor Greek, slave nor free, and no "male and female" (in other words, no longer any privileging of the male through the sign of circumcision, since females are baptized, and called to faith, equally with males) because you are "all one in Messiah Jesus". All of this means a large area of *adiaphora*, which as we shall presently see needs to be worked out through wise pastoral advice. Equally, the creational and covenantal monotheism which lies at the heart of both Jewish and Christian faith, and is not diluted by Paul's view of Jesus and the Spirit but is rather put into dramatic and decisive operation through that view, is radically maintained, and with it the clear, high calling to a sexual and marital standard which, as with Jesus himself in Mark 10, reflects the original creative purpose.

For Paul, as I just hinted, Jewish-style monotheism was radically reinterpreted through Jesus and the Spirit. The hope of Israel – that the divine glory would be revealed for "all flesh" to see, with Zion's watchmen shouting for joy as the glorious presence returned at last to the city and the Temple – had been radically fulfilled, in a way nobody had anticipated, in the person of Jesus himself and in the presence, power and leading of the Spirit. In 2 Corinthians 3 and 4

Paul expounds the story of the coming of the divine presence into the wilderness tabernacle in Exodus 32–34, and explains it in terms both of the transforming presence of the Spirit and of "the light of the knowledge of the glory of God in the face of Jesus the Messiah". In Galatians 4 the slave-rescuing God is the one who sends the Son and then sends the Spirit of the Son, resulting in the remarkable claim, "Now that you know God, or rather have been known by God", and the very Jewish, anti-pagan challenge, "How can you turn back to the weak and beggarly 'elements'?" In Romans 8, the redemptive work accomplished through the sending of God's own Son is then applied through the Spirit's work, "leading" the people to their "inheritance" – in other words, doing in the "new Exodus" what the strange divine presence in cloud and fire had done in the first Exodus. For Paul, the events of Messiah and Spirit have explicated and shaped afresh what it means to believe in the One God.

Exactly these elements have also contributed directly to the reshaping of the Jewish belief that marital and sexual behaviour is closely allied to belief in the One Creator God. Paul's instructions about behaviour in these areas are emphatically "in the Lord", worked out particularly in the remarkable Christological analogy for husband and wife in Ephesians 5. The basis for the rejection of pagan sexual behaviour and the embrace of a new way of life (a way which that great pagan, the doctor Galen, recognized as strange to the point of madness in terms of the "normal" behavioural standards of his world) is that "you were washed, sanctified and justified in the name of the Lord, Messiah Jesus, and in the Spirit of our God" (1 Corinthians 6:11). Unity with the Messiah is what matters, and this will be radically compromised by *porneia* (6:15–17). The body that has been "an expensive purchase" – in other words, that has been redeemed through the blood of the Messiah – is now "a temple of the Holy Spirit" (6:19). The closing command of that decisive chapter, "glorify God in your body" (6:20), is not simply about "honouring" God in the way one behaves. It is about recognizing, and "giving glory to", the God who has purchased the body through the person and death of the Son, and who now indwells the body through the person and power of the Spirit. This is a Trinitarian ethic flowing directly from the Trinitarian reworking of monotheism itself (as in 1 Corinthians 12:4–6 and elsewhere).

For Paul, therefore, there is continuity with the ancient Jewish worship and ethic, and there is also enhancement. The same God; the same standard; but now this God is revealed in radically fresh ways through Jesus and the Spirit, and the standard is clarified and energized by that same revelation-in-action. This, for Paul, is foundational.

It ought now to be clear, before we proceed, that we cannot get to the heart of Paul's thinking in these or related areas through the old supposition that he merely opposed "works of the law" – a category which, for many interpreters, included circumcision and food taboos on the one hand and matters of personal behaviour on the other in an undifferentiated agglomeration. There was nothing wrong with the Jewish law, as Paul makes clear in various passages. The differentiation he introduces has nothing to do with deciding that some parts of Torah are good and to be retained (sexual ethics) and other parts are bad and to be abolished (food laws, circumcision, and so on). That is not the point. The point is, again, *messianic eschatology*: the Messiah has come, and in his death, resurrection, and sending of the Spirit he has inaugurated the new age, the new covenant, the new creation. Some parts of Torah – the parts which kept Israel separate from the Gentile world until the coming of Messiah – have done their work and are now put to one side, not because they were bad but because they were good and have done their work. Other parts of Torah – the parts which pointed to the divine intention to renew the whole creation through Israel – are celebrated as being now at last within reach through Jesus and the Spirit. The old has passed away; all things have become new – and the "new" includes the triumphant and celebratory recovery of the original created intention, not least for male and female in marriage.

Of course here, too (notably in 1 Corinthians 7), Paul introduces a further radical proposal: that, against the assumption and the attempted legislation of the day, widows were free *not* to remarry, and singleness (and hence childlessness) was a valid and appropriate state for those who were called to it. Marriage thus witnesses to the recovery of the original creative intention; singleness (including staying single after either divorce or widowhood) to the fact that the ultimate "new creation" is yet to come. There is thus a "now and not yet" element to Paul's ethic of marriage and singleness, which again is not captured by any suggestion that he is either "for" or "against" something called "the law", seen as a collection of miscellaneous instructions. He has gone far deeper than that. His vision of the church is a vision of the Messiah himself, defeating sin and death and thereby fulfilling Israel's vocation of being the answer to the problems of the wider world. That vision is then implemented through the Spirit, calling into being through the gospel a new-covenant, new-creation people. Because this people is the new-*covenant* people, the temporary regulations of the old covenant are set aside as having done their job. Because this people is the new-*creation* people, the creational vision of the One God with his image-bearing male-and-female humans is enhanced, rescued from decay, and brought within reach. If we still sense this as a paradox, that may be an indication that we have not yet come to terms with the depths of Paul's reading of Scripture in the light of the crucified and risen Messiah and the gift and power of the Spirit.

Paul's vision of unity and *adiaphora*

It should by now be clear that when Paul appeals for unity across traditional boundaries, and for the consequent rendering as *adiaphora* of cultural taboos which up to that point have been mandatory, this owes nothing to any sense that, in the new dispensation, one can play fast and loose with fussy old regulations. That is not the point. What we see in the two crucial passages, Romans 14–15 and 1 Corinthians

8–10, is the principled and also pastorally sensitive application of his belief that in the Messiah and by the Spirit a new, multi-ethnic people has come into existence in surprising fulfilment of ancient promises.

The two passages are subtly different; we may take Romans 14–15 first. I hold the view that here Paul is addressing the problem that in Rome there are several house churches, between which there exist significant variations in practice regarding food, drink, and holy days. This is only to be expected. There may be some Jewish–Christian groups in Rome who still, like their Jerusalem counterparts, see all of Torah as mandatory, while some Gentile–Christian groups have known from the start that their own admission to the Messiah's people is not on the basis of Torah. Equally, there may be Jewish Christians who, like Paul himself (and quite possibly under his teaching), have come to see that Torah, though good and God-given, has in significant ways been set aside as the marker of the eschatologically renewed people. And there may be some Gentile Christians who, like some of the ex-pagans in Galatia, have been so delighted with what they have discovered of the Jewish and biblical context of the Messiah's work that they have been eager to embrace even those parts of Jewish tradition that, in Paul's view at least, are no longer relevant now that the Messiah has died and been raised, and that the Spirit has been poured out. And this is just a start. There may be many more variations, rooted both in ethnic traditions and identities and in different understandings of the gospel and its significance.

Paul's aim throughout this section of Romans, as becomes clear in 15:7–13, is *united worship*, rooted in mutual respect. He does not here ask the different groups to give up their practices; merely not to judge one another where differences exist. As Paul well knew (though we sometimes forget), this is actually just as large a step, if not larger, than a change in practice itself. *The move from regarding something as mandatory to regarding it as optional is vast*, just as vast in fact as *the move from regarding something as forbidden to regarding it as available*. Even if one is not going to take advantage of the "optional" clause in the first of these, or the "available" clause in the second, admitting that it might be so is the main thing. (That, of course, is why the apparently innocuous "live and let live" proposals for reform are the real crunch, as most reforming groups know well.)

Paul sometimes appears to relish the ironies which result. Neither circumcision nor uncircumcision matters, he says in 1 Corinthians 7:19, since what really matters is *keeping God's commandments* – fully aware, of course, that the command to circumcise was basic in Torah. And here, as the necessary pastoral outworking of this principle, Paul introduces the vital messianic principle: if your brother or sister is being injured by what you eat, you are no longer walking in love; you might, by your exercise of freedom, "destroy someone for whom the Messiah died" (14:15). This must then be correlated with the principle of conscience: if you have thought through what you are doing, and understand why it is right for you, then go ahead; but to act while doubting, in other words not from faith, is to sin (14:23).

This whole discussion alerts us to the fact that Paul is here applying pastoral wisdom to contentious situations. He knows perfectly well that people cannot change the habits of a lifetime overnight, including the kinds of food they eat or do not eat. He knows that there will therefore be within the church many people living side by side whose "natural" way of doing things will be different from one another. Here the principles of charity on the one hand (not destroying a sibling for whom the Messiah died) and conscience on the other (acting from thought-out faith) must inform what is done. Messiah-people will make demands on one another's charity; they must not make demands on one another's conscience. This does not, to be sure, produce a fixed and balanced policy that will last a generation. Things will change over time as people think things through afresh, as new members of the body arrive from elsewhere bringing with them their own expectations and sensitivities. The rules of charity and conscience are there, not to nail down a one-size-fits-all rule-book but precisely to enable mutual respect and shared worship in the absence of such a thing. But – and we should note this once again – Paul does *not* apply this to questions of sexual ethics (or for that matter to extortion, murder, violence, lying, mutual lawsuits, and so forth). In this passage, he has made that abundantly clear in 13:11–14, before the present discussion can get under way – perhaps deliberately warding off any misunderstandings in advance.

A similar pattern may be observed in 1 Corinthians 8–10, where Paul's dealing with serious sexual misdemeanour in chapter 5 ("Drive out the wicked person from your company") has led to a more general warning against *porneia* in chapter 6, and then the wider instructions about marriage, divorce, and singleness in chapter 7. It is as though he needs to get clear on all this before he can begin to address the issues which are indeed to be considered *adiaphora* – though, to be sure, the question of a Christian's relation to idol temples in a city like Corinth was not detached from questions of *porneia*.

The issue at stake in chapters 8, 9, and 10 is not quite the same as that in Romans 14 and 15. There, Paul was faced with various different groups, most likely in different house churches, probably reflecting different aspects of their ethnic backgrounds. Here, in 1 Corinthians, there is one church – albeit prone to factionalism! – and the issue is more focused. Granted that virtually all the meat offered for sale in a city like Corinth would have already been offered in an idol temple, does that mean it is all "off limits"? Is it irrevocably "tainted"?

Paul goes right to the heart of the issue, with his Christologically redefined Jewish monotheism. There are many so-called "gods" and "lords", but they are a sham: for us "there is one God, the Father, from whom are all things and [literally] we to him, and one Lord, Jesus the Messiah, through whom are all things and [literally] we through him". Paul has reworked the ancient daily Jewish prayer, the *Shema*, and has discerned Jesus at its heart. Monotheism is his main point, here and in the concluding summary when he quotes a similarly emphatic text, Psalm 24:1 ("the earth is the Lord's, and all its fullness"). Here too Jesus is at least implied, as it often is when Paul quotes the Septuagint *kyrios* ("Lord").

From this Jewish-style and Jesus-focused monotheism (very different from the pantheistic "monotheism" of the Stoics) two things follow. First, the idols themselves have no real existence. Zeus, Athene, Mars, Aphrodite, and the rest are figments of human imagination. Meat offered to them therefore does not "belong" to them: a non-existent being cannot own things. It still belongs to the One true God, and it can be eaten if received with thanksgiving. Second, however, when humans worship these non-gods they are actually getting in touch with, and giving power to, the *daimonia* – nasty, shadowy little non-human beings who hang out in the idol temples like ill-kempt squatters camping in a great mansion. These beings, though in no way "divine", nevertheless have a power, stolen perhaps from the humans who worship the "gods" (this is one of the points we wish Paul had made a bit clearer), which can not only mess up human lives but, more importantly, puts them as it were in competition with the lordship of Jesus himself. Someone who belongs to the Messiah but who actually goes into an idol shrine and eats and drinks there is by strong implication playing off the Messiah against the *daimonia*, and vice versa.

Paul's main point, then, is that to buy the meat in the market, or to eat it when invited to someone's home, is absolutely fine. But to go into an idol temple and share in the meal on offer there is not. In Ben Witherington's characteristic phrase, "it is more a matter of venue than menu".[1] That is the basic framework of his argument, thought out clearly on the basis of the Christologically reimagined monotheism.

The key question for Paul is then, "How does this apply pastorally in a church where many members have in the past frequented idol temples and shared in the entire way of life that they embody?" For some, we may suppose – reading between Paul's lines, but only a little – the very smell of cooked meat might easily conjure up the sights and sounds, incense wafting around idolatrous statues, boys and girls working the crowd to offer sexual favours, another glass of wine, then another, and then... bad memories, a dark mixture of thrill and guilt, a soul steadily eroded, a sense of chaos only warded off by more of the same. That was what the Messiah had rescued them from! Why would they want to have anything to do with it again?

Paul designates these two positions the "strong" and the "weak". The "strong" know that all meat is available to them; the "weak" will find that it puts a strain on their conscience. We must remember, reading this terminology, that in writing to the Corinthians in particular he insists that the Messiah's cross has redefined power in terms of "weakness", so we must not imagine that these terms carry a kind of superiority complex in which the "strong" (Paul himself included) can look down their noses at the "weak" who should really, they might think, get their act together. Certainly not. As in Romans 14, these are siblings for whom the Messiah died (1 Corinthians 8:11). And here we come to the heart of Paul's doctrine of *adiaphora*. Meat – in this case, food that has been offered to idols – is not to be a community-divider. It all belongs to the One God. But for that to be a reality – for the community not to be divided – all parties must see that what matters is not the meat itself *but the conscience of the person who might or might not eat*. Paul even, unusually for him, enters into some detailed situational discussion: if a pagan invites you to dinner, go and eat without raising questions, but if someone says "Don't you realise that was offered to an idol" you should abstain (1 Corinthians 10:27–30), not because of your conscience, but because of theirs.

This, then, is how the *adiaphora* rule works. First, the robust Trinitarian monotheism now made known through Jesus and the Spirit is basic, enhancing and explaining further the essential Jewish monotheism in which all creation is good (in other words, Paul is a million miles away from Platonic dualism, still more from Gnosticism). Those who have had scruples about this or that need to think through what this Christ-and-Spirit-shaped monotheism means in practice. Second, that will take time, because humans do not always change mental and practical habits overnight, and in this case they should not be forced to do so. But in a mixed community, where people are still "on the way" in being taught, in prayerfully thinking this through, the "strong" should defer to the "weak". This again neither reflects nor produces a stable situation. Opinions may change, different community members may take different positions, and there is always the awkward moment when, sitting in good conscience at someone's table, a bystander makes a comment which indicates a "weak" conscience. As often, Paul is not legislating for all situations, nor could he. He is teaching people *to think messianically*, and especially to think through their own faith and practice, and their membership of the community with others on the same journey but at different points along the road, in the light of the Messiah's death and resurrection. He is teaching them to *navigate* through difficult and only partly charted waters, with the Messiah and his saving death as the principal star by which they must steer. And in that situation the subtle rule of *adiaphora* is about as different from a modern doctrine of "tolerance" as can be imagined. "Tolerance" is not simply a low-grade version of "love"; in some senses, it is its opposite, as "tolerance" can imply a distancing, a wave from the other side of the street, rather than the rich embrace of "the sibling for whom the Messiah died".

Conclusion

There is much more, of course, that could and perhaps should be said about Paul and *adiaphora*. What matters is that we grasp as firmly as we can the fundamental principles of ecclesiology which Paul not only articulated as theory but worked out in pastoral and epistolary practice. To understand the church as the Messiah's Spirit-filled people, and as such as the community of new covenant and new creation, is to understand the difference between the matters in relation to which the church can and must live with difference of practice and the matters in relation to which the church has neither right nor mandate to approve or condone such differences. We, of course, live in a world where, in the aftermath of the Enlightenment's watering down of Reformation theology, many have reduced the faith to a set of abstract doctrines and a list of detached and apparently arbitrary rules, which "conservatives" then insist upon and "radicals" try to bend or merely ignore. It is this framework itself which we have got wrong, resulting in dialogues of the deaf or, worse, the lobbing of angry verbal hand grenades over walls of incomprehension. Paul's framework was very different. It may be painful for us to learn to think within his framework rather than the one into which we regularly fall. But only if we learn to do so will we understand, and be able to navigate, the real challenges we face today and tomorrow.

***

Questions

1. Paul calls the church to both unity and holiness. Do you tend to favour one or the other? Have you experienced them to be in tension?

2. What in Paul's vision of the church challenges our common understanding? How does it help us to address our disagreements better?

3. Why does Paul draw such a close link between belief and behaviour?

4. How does Paul's teaching about new creation and new covenant help us to distinguish between differences which don't matter (*adiaphora*) and differences which do.

5. How can the categories of "strong" and "weak" help us to disagree better?

5

Good Disagreement and the Reformation

Ashley Null

The sixteenth-century Reformation is famous as an age of religious division, between Roman Catholic and Protestant, and between numerous Protestant groups, which continues to shape Western Christianity today. But it was also, surprisingly, an era of consensus building. Theologians like John Calvin and Thomas Cranmer hammered out major questions concerning the essentials of the faith, religious tolerance, and confessional unity. In this chapter, historian Ashley Null delves into the Reformation debates for signs of "good disagreement".

Confessional identities

After almost 500 years of living with confessional divisions within Western Christianity, it is easy to forget that these separate Christian identities are the product of the Reformation, not its cause. In the beginning, all those involved were simply Catholic Christians seeking to be faithful to what that meant. Traditionalists relied primarily on the medieval church for direction, whereas the reformers looked back to the primitive church instead. Because they could not agree on what it meant to be a good Catholic, their differences eventually led to the development of the divisions we know today as Roman Catholic, Lutheran, Anabaptist, Reformed, and Anglican, as well as many further Protestant options. Since Western Christianity is now defined by these centuries-long confessional consequences, the Reformation is often characterized as an era of "bad disagreement".

After all, disagreement over doctrine too many times led to death. Roman Catholics burned Protestants as heretics, filling John Foxe's famous *Book of Martyrs* with countless stirring accounts of ordinary people dying for Reformation faith. Protestants, in turn, burned reformers whom they felt went too far and abandoned creedal Christianity entirely, like the incarnation-denying Joan Bocher in Thomas Cranmer's England or the anti-Trinitarian Michael Servetus in John Calvin's Geneva. When religious fervour was used to mobilize popular forces against the government, rulers across the confessional divide did not hesitate to use the bloody sword of state to suppress rebellion, whether it be as early as Thomas Müntzer and the Peasants' Revolt in the 1520s, or as late as the Jesuit missionaries in England who rejected Elizabeth I as queen in the 1580s.

The initial confessional dividing line was drawn over the authority to determine doctrine. On the one hand, conservative Catholics insisted that only the leadership of the church could interpret the Bible, since medieval scholasticism had stressed the authority of the church's teaching tradition as expressed in its highest forms through church councils and the office of the pope. On the other, reforming Catholics beginning with Martin Luther argued that Scripture as its own interpreter must be the ultimate authority in doctrinal matters. The essentials of salvation were clear for anyone to understand, and more difficult biblical passages needed to be understood in the light of other passages on the same topic which were easier to grasp. Since reforming Catholics believed Scripture taught a very different understanding of the way of salvation and the nature of the sacraments than the medieval church had decreed, they sought to renew the Catholic Church by bringing it back to its ancient truths. Luther called this movement for reformation in Germany "*evangelisch*" because of its emphasis on the biblical message. Hence, reforming Catholics became known in English as gospellers or evangelicals.

Yet, as the reformation movement progressed, additional confessional lines began to be drawn between evangelicals. Enthusiasts arose who placed more authority in what the Spirit was telling them individually to do through prophetic utterances than what the Spirit had written in the Bible. Emphasizing the importance of professing personal faith, they also rejected the baptism of infants. Other radical reformers renounced any involvement with secular authorities, including involvement in their court systems, serving in their armies, or even swearing oaths, which was an integral part of normal everyday life. Some of these Anabaptists decided to enter into communal living, sharing all their possessions. Luther and the other "magisterial" reformers would have nothing to do with the radicals.

However, confessional lines also emerged within the mainstream Reformation movement. The initial source of this division was over the nature of Christ's presence in Holy Communion. Reforming Catholics could not agree on how to interpret the phrase "This is my body". Was "is" to be taken literally or figuratively? If the search for unity between conservative and reforming Catholics centred on deciding how the Bible was to be interpreted in general, the search for unity among reforming Catholics (soon to be called Protestants) focused on how this particular Bible passage was to be understood. Despite the ultimate failure to reconcile any of these differences, the Reformation should still not be written off as an era of only "bad disagreements". Ironic as it may seem, the confessional identities which still divide Western Christianity today are, in fact, the enduring result of that era's successful attempts at "good disagreement", if only within specific streams.

The humanist background

Despite the church-given mandate to promote intellectual unity, medieval universities did the opposite. By promoting disputations which used competing logical arguments to test the probability of intellectual possibilities, their scholastic method created rival schools of thought on various philosophical and theological questions. Although the medieval dream of intellectual unity was never lost, it was never realized either. As a result, in fourteenth-century Italy Petrarch became one of the first scholars to turn to humanism as a better way to unity. In his opinion, Aristotelian scholasticism only led to vanity, obstinacy, and a multiplication of sects, which resulted in quarrels, ambiguity, and an entangling confusion of words which was of no use. Petrarch's solution was to restrict the search for truth to the things necessary for salvation as taught by divine revelation so people could concentrate on leading good lives.[1]

At the beginning of the sixteenth century, the Dutch scholar Erasmus decided to walk in the footsteps of Petrarch. Practical morality was far more important to Erasmus than detailed doctrinal debates. Hence, he rejected the scholastic pursuit of "frivolous questions". Instead, his "philosophy of Christ" looked to Scripture not only to establish the certitudes necessary for how a Christian should live but also to inflame its readers with a supernatural love for God so that they would desire to act accordingly.[2] Hence, Erasmus delighted in contrasting the tedious, confusing technical jargon which scholasticism produced to Christ's clear moral imperative to do good deeds found in the Bible. Since he emphasized Scripture's ethical certitudes as the only sure basis for Christian unity, Erasmus felt comfortable in outlining the ancient options among various less important intellectual possibilities without feeling the need to come to a definitive conclusion. Thus, his humanism was able to conceive of "good disagreement" in things not essential for Christian unity as defined by the biblical way of salvation.

Martin Luther and religious tolerance

Of course, Erasmian peacemaking in the face of religious difference was premised on two assumptions: (1) that the basic principles of salvation were universally recognized; and (2) that the most important factor was fulfilling Christ's moral teaching in cooperation with divine assistance. Looking to the writings of Paul, Luther radically redefined justification as being passively received by faith rather than actively achieved through working with divine grace. In so doing, he rejected the fundamental medieval principle of cooperation with God and made certainty about God's redemptive action for the believer absolutely crucial instead. Thus, Luther directly challenged Erasmus's moralist approach to Christian renewal in favour of a new certainty in God's biblical promises, as their testy exchange in 1524–25 over divine sovereignty and "the bondage of the will" made clear. With the advent of the Protestant Reformation, Europe was now riven by competing claims for saving truth.

At first, Luther had little concern for how his gospel preaching affected political unity. Stressing the clear separation between the spiritual sphere and the political in his teaching on the two distinct governments of church and society, Luther insisted that God himself brought about true Christian belief through the preaching of the gospel of the forgiveness of sins. Consequently, saving faith could not be coerced by the sword. State power simply had no role in regulating the consciences of its subjects, only their outward conduct for the sake of society. Hence, individuals were free to believe as they saw fit, as long as they lived in accordance with the state's laws designed for the common good.

In the early years of the Reformation, Luther was even prepared to extend this toleration of dissent to Jews. Rather than the typical argument for forced conversion or expulsion, his 1523 treatise *Jesus Christ was Born a Jew* made a revolutionary call for Jewish integration. Jews should live unhindered among their Christian neighbours. They should be admitted to all vocations, and in a parallel writing Luther even argued for the possibility of Jewish–Christian intermarriage. In short, because the state had neither need for nor right over people's consciences, whatever kind of Christian or Jew they might be, Luther urged the creation of a society tolerant of religious diversity.

Nevertheless, his call went unheeded by political leaders, and two events of the mid-1520s would shortly make clear the full implications of his teaching on the two governments. The Peasants' War of 1525 demonstrated to Luther the duty of princes to suppress those who fomented violence in the name of the gospel, since the peasants claimed divine sanction for their rebellion against their political overlords. And in the face of the poor condition of the Saxon church, his 1527 visitation of local parishes showed him the practical necessity of institutional government support for the Reformation's consolidation and advancement.

Although Luther was careful to stress that the government should not overstep its authority in church matters, he decided that a prince's duty to preserve peace and maintain the common good now extended to establishing outward religious conformity. While princes could not compel faith, they needed to restrict external abominations. Henceforth, deviations from state-sanctioned ecclesiastical practices were seen as a threat to the common good and required punishment by the sword. Although the mature Luther continued to teach his doctrine of the two governments, he nevertheless returned to the traditional model of a Christian commonwealth, complete with an institutionalized ecclesiastical monopoly. Thus, he could no longer envision "good disagreement" about the essential nature of true religion.

Protestant divisions over the Lord's Supper

Luther soon learned that state-sanctioned support for the evangelical cause brought with it political pressure for doctrinal unity among its leading theologians. Emperor Charles V was a committed Roman Catholic who openly opposed Luther after his excommunication. Although the Diet of Worms (1521) issued an edict making the Reformation illegal, political circumstances for many years prevented the emperor from using military action to enforce it. After a few years of official permission for princes and cities to do what they thought best in matters of religion, the Diet of Speyer in 1529 sharply renewed pressure on the Reformation movement. In Roman Catholic lands the Edict of Worms was to be fully enforced so as to give no new foothold for Lutheranism. But, on the other hand, in areas with a Lutheran majority no further evangelical progress was permitted, and Roman Catholics were to be allowed to practise their faith as well and attend mass unhindered. The evangelical rulers immediately objected that it was not possible to govern a land in peace and quiet if such religious diversity were permitted. Since the previous policy had been passed unanimously, the evangelicals argued that it could not now be overturned by a mere majority. Because of their protest, the dissenters – a mere five princes and fourteen cities out of about 400 in the Holy Roman Empire – were henceforth called "Protestants".

Well aware of their minority status, the Lutheran rulers immediately after Speyer began to work towards a military defence league. Philip, Landgrave of Hesse, sought to unite all the evangelicals from Switzerland to Denmark in a grand coalition to partner with France to stand up to Charles V, a mighty ruler of vast territories in Europe and the New World. Luther was not convinced that it was either Christian or even legal to form a federation against the supreme sovereign in the empire. His normal preference was to resist authorities with words rather than weapons and then suffer passively should the state sword be drawn. Yet there was an even bigger obstacle to his endorsement of the Landgrave's plan. Luther always considered political needs secondary to questions of theological truth, and he and the Swiss evangelicals had already been engaged in a very public "Supper-strife" over the nature of Christ's presence in Holy Communion. In order to demonstrate unity in Reformation doctrine, Philip had to foster agreement to a common confession. Therefore, he invited all the major evangelical theologians to his castle at Marburg for a colloquy in October 1529.

Although reluctant to attend since he saw little hope of agreement, Luther bowed to the wishes of his prince that he go and make the best of it. He and Philipp Melanchthon came from Saxony, Huldrych Zwingli from Zürich, Johannes Oecolampadius from Basel, Martin Bucer from Strassburg, Johannes Brenz from Schwäbisch-Hall, and Andreas Osiander from Nürnberg. They engaged in four days of intense debate, seeking theological consensus. Luther insisted that Jesus' phrase, "This is my body", should be interpreted literally; consequently, Christ's human body was truly present in the Supper in a mystical fashion. Zwingli and Oecolampadius were equally determined that it should be understood figuratively, for they interpreted Jesus' words at the Last Supper in the light of John 6:63, "The Spirit gives life, the flesh counts for nothing." Hence, the only kind of life-giving eating of Christ in the Supper had to be spiritual, not carnal. Luther argued, however, that this passage had to be understood in the light of Jesus' words at the Last Supper and not the other way around, for if the flesh always counted for nothing, then the incarnation itself had no value. After some prodding by the Landgrave, both sides eventually agreed to fourteen articles. The fifteenth article, however, admitted their continuing stalemate about the Lord's Supper. Although both sides disavowed transubstantiation and recognized that its benefits were received spiritually for the building up of faith, the participants could not agree on the manner of Christ's presence. Their hopes for a unified Protestant front faltered on this one point.

In the light of their agreement on the essentials of the faith in fourteen and a half articles, Philip and Bucer (who was closer to Zwingli than Luther) were eager for both sides to agree to disagree about the presence. They wanted everyone to call one another "brother" and so engage in intercommunion. After all, both northern German territories like Hesse and southern German cities like Strassburg had signed the protest in Speyer together. Luther, however, rejected any attempt to make the nature of the Lord's Supper a secondary issue. He would not fellowship with those who rejected something as essential to saving faith as Jesus' own words about his incarnated presence. Luther bluntly informed Bucer that he had another spirit.

When the emperor asked the German Protestants in 1530 to give an account of their religious practices, Melanchthon was deputized to take up the cause on behalf of the northern evangelicals. Whereas Erasmus sought Christian unity based on Christ's moral teaching, Melanchthon designed the Augsburg Confession as an appeal for Christian unity based on the agreed essentials of salvation by grace through faith for Christ's sake. Scripture, not the church's teaching tradition, was the ultimate authority to determine what those doctrinal essentials were. Yet, the confession not only detailed the Protestants' understanding of salvation. In keeping with the precedent set by Luther at Marburg, Melanchthon incorporated a real presence understanding of the Lord's Supper as one of the "chief articles of faith". Because they disagreed with this part of the Augsburg Confession, Bucer and the south German cities were forced to submit a separate doctrinal statement which steered a middle course between the northern Germans and the Swiss. In the end, neither was accepted by the emperor. As for the Swiss, they were completely on their own, with Zwingli dying in battle the next year, sword in hand. By the beginning of the 1530s, northern German, southern German, and Swiss evangelicals were united in their opposition to Rome and to one another.

Essentials and *adiaphora*

Because of Luther's stand at Marburg, Protestants could not even agree on how to rank the importance of their disagreements. If the best hope for Christian, or at least Protestant, unity lay in an emphasis on gospel essentials, the key question for the remainder of the Reformation period was what exactly were those essentials and how were they determined? The remarkable level of agreement at Marburg was not sufficient in Luther's eyes for either eucharistic fellowship or even a military pact. Bucer, however, argued that all those who preached forgiveness through justification by faith alone and practised loving their neighbour were clearly Christians who could and should share fellowship. His position was well known in Antwerp, where two of England's earliest evangelicals, William Tyndale and John Frith, lived and worked together on a vernacular English Bible. Frith had even attended the colloquy at Marburg. Both Englishmen sided with the Swiss rather than Luther on the nature of the eucharistic presence, and both sided with Bucer that the presence was an *adiaphoron* – that is, a thing "indifferent", not essential for Christian unity.

After Frith made a missionary journey back to England in 1532 to encourage underground evangelical circles, Tyndale wrote a letter offering his thoughts on how to proceed. Concerning the Lord's Supper, Tyndale advised against giving unnecessary offence to Lutherans:

> *Of the presence of Christ's body in the sacrament, meddle as little as you can, that there appear no division among us... I would have the right use preached, and the presence to be an indifferent thing, till the matter might be reasoned in peace at leisure of both parties.*[3]

Tyndale expected that his advice would be well received, because Frith's commitment to major only on the majors was one of the things Tyndale most admired about his younger colleague. He described Frith as someone who stuck stubbornly to the necessary things of the gospel which were taught in Scripture, while avoiding getting entangled in debates about secondary things which "neither help or hinder".[4]

At the time he penned his missive, Tyndale was unaware that Frith had already been imprisoned for his theological views. Yet, Tyndale had not misjudged his colleague. Frith was burned at the stake not for rejecting transubstantiation *per se*, but rather for insisting that the nature of Christ's eucharistic presence was itself an *adiaphoron*. In his *Answer to Sir Thomas More*, Frith justified his tolerance position by arguing that only articles of the Apostles' Creed were necessary to be believed for salvation. Indeed, he asserted that those who were being condemned as heretics were never guilty of rejecting any part of the creed, but were being "put to death because they say that we are not bound to believe every point that the laws and tyranny of the clergy allow and maintain".[5]

Tyndale echoed both Bucer and Frith on the nature of Christian essentials. The law, the prophets, and Jesus had but one point: to bring people to believe in Christ for the forgiveness of their sins and love their neighbour as a result.

> *Therefore methinketh that the party that hath professed the faith of Christ, and the love of his neighbour, ought of duty to bear each other, as long as the other opinion is not plain wicked through false idolatry, nor contrary to the salvation that is in Christ, nor against the open and manifest doctrine of Christ and his apostles, nor contrary to the general articles of the faith of the general church of Christ, which are confirmed with open scripture, in which articles never a true church in any land dissenteth.*[6]

On the one hand, since those who did not believe in the bodily presence of Christ still trusted Christ for forgiveness and loved their enemies for his sake, they clearly had the Spirit of Christ at work within them. "Why then should they," Tyndale asked, "that boast themselves to be Christ's friends, slay them?" On the other hand, since the doctrine of transubstantiation did not contradict the normative standards of Scripture and the creeds, Tyndale was willing, "for unity's sake", to accept this teaching as a viable Christian option.[7]

In the end, the sticking point with transubstantiation was not so much the doctrine itself, but its use to promote what Tyndale considered to be idolatrous ceremonies. Abuses like the mass as a sacrifice for sin, or prayers directed to the sacrament instead of heavenward, actually undermined true faith and love. Of course, trusting in human works like the mass to bring about the forgiveness of sins denied justification by faith alone. Yet, no greater evidence of the corrupting power of these practices was needed than "blind zeal" for opinions that "neither letteth nor hindereth to salvation" which led its Catholic defenders to lose all love for their neighbours to the point of killing them.[8] Thus, by separating transubstantiation from its abusive ceremonies, Frith and Tyndale were able to declare the doctrine an "indifferent thing". Some later reformers would reverse that logic; namely, they would refuse to declare certain ceremonies *adiaphora* because they feared that such practices would lead to the unscriptural belief in transubstantiation.

Building consensus

In the end, Bucer realized that with Luther's consistent stand, the way to German Protestant unity would not be through an adiaphorist approach to Christ's presence in the Lord's Supper. Convinced that ultimately no matter of importance separated the Swiss and German descriptions on such a holy mystery, he worked tirelessly to find a verbal formula satisfactory to both the northern and southern German Protestants. Much to the horror of his Swiss colleagues, he publicly endorsed the Augsburg Confession in 1532, for Bucer had agreed to redefine his understanding of "spiritual presence" to mean a post-resurrection mystical presence where Christ's human body was no longer restricted by normal physical laws and, thus, Jesus was present in both body and spirit. Although Bucer was never trusted again by the Swiss, his willingness to embrace some kind of physical presence opened the way for further negotiations with Luther. The fruit of these discussions was the Wittenberg Concord (1536), a carefully worded statement that enabled both sides to concentrate on what they considered to be the essentials on this issue, while quietly passing over in silence a major disagreement.

Fundamental to Luther was the Lord's Supper being God's gift to his people, not a human offering to him. Like the salvation which it proclaimed, the Supper was God's action received by the people. Of course that act was Christ's full self-giving, both his divinity and humanity. Fundamental to Bucer was that in the sacrament, as in salvation, people participated in Christ only through faith. Once Luther had been assured by the southern German participants individually that they believed that Christ's body and blood were "truly and substantially" present, two sticking points remained. First, Luther associated Christ's self-giving with the elements themselves, whereas Bucer preferred to avoid localizing the presence in them. Second, Bucer denied that non-believers, lacking faith, received Christ, whereas Luther insisted that Christ was present to all, although only to the condemnation of non-believers. For, according to Luther, God's act in giving the objective presence of Christ made a believer's reception possible. A believer's act of faith did not make the reception of the presence of Christ possible – that would render a divine gift merely a human work. The careful wording of the Wittenberg Concord found a way through both issues.

On the one hand, Christ was described as giving himself through a sacramental union "with" the elements, not "in" the elements. On the other, it was affirmed that the "unworthy" experienced the presence of Christ, rather than "unbelievers". The ambiguity implicit in the new word had the advantage of allowing each side to interpret it according to his own view. For Bucer, "unworthy" meant only Christian believers, since only those with faith could participate in Christ, yet as sinners justified by faith rather than their own works, they were still not inherently worthy of the gift. For Luther, however, "unworthy" meant both believers and non-believers, since all humanity was unworthy of the divine gift of Christ's objective presence. Deciding that "unworthy" was sufficient to safeguard participation in the Supper from becoming a human work, Luther was willing for the statement to make no explicit pronouncement on the divisive issue of non-believers, effectively treating it as an *adiaphoron*. Having secured a commitment from the southern Germans to a corporeal presence, Luther accepted both of these concessions to Bucer as sufficient for intercommunion. In so doing, Luther had agreed to disagree about important aspects of the theological explanation of the real presence for the sake of unity.

Here is the best example of him as a mature reformer engaging in "good disagreement".

Unfortunately, Luther's sincere attempt at unity only led to further "bad disagreement". Zürich stoutly refused to accept the Wittenberg Concord because of its use of the word "substantially". Feeling betrayed by Bucer, they hardened their stance against the real presence. In turn, their rejection brought out in the older Luther some of his harshest language ever against fellow evangelicals. His thundering denunciations of the Swiss sacramental doctrine in the 1540s heightened the tensions between the two groups. As a result, Calvin of Geneva reached out to Heinrich Bullinger, Zwingli's successor as chief pastor of Zürich, to see if their two Swiss cities could take the lead in working out an agreement. Since Bucer was Calvin's mentor, Calvin was closer to Luther's view, whereas Bullinger was faithful to the later Zwingli who after Marburg spoke more often of a spiritual presence at the Supper, rather than a mere memorial meal. Because of his relationship with Bucer, it took Calvin five years, epistolary persistence, Bucerian attention to language, and a surprise visit to overcome Bullinger's wariness of his approaches and reach an accord. Yet, the resulting Zürich Agreement (*Consensus Tigurinus*), signed in 1549, became the enduring foundation for subsequent reformed sacramental theology, even if not the universal Reformation position as they had hoped for.

Like his mentor Bucer, Calvin prized Christian unity, and he was prepared in his discussions with Bullinger to seek a verbal formula that both sides could live with in good conscience. As a result, neither side got a full description of their views enshrined in the accord, but both sides could point to enough of their fundamental sacramental principles to be comfortable with the result. Ever determined to refuse to tie divine activity explicitly to creaturely things, Bullinger's essentials included the clear denial of any kind of real corporal presence, for Jesus' words at the Last Supper were figurative, not literal. He also denied any direct association between the elements and the work of the Spirit in the hearts of the elect. Calvin, on the other hand, sought to strengthen the link between Christ's action and sacramental participation. He would have preferred to have included "substantially" as well as emphasize the connection between the elements and the spiritual gifts being imparted. Yet, he was willing to agree to Bullinger's non-negotiables, so long as the accord clearly taught Christ's spiritual presence in the heart of the believer and the sacrament as a means to deepen union with Christ. For the sake of unity, Bullinger was willing to agree to some language which suggested that God used the sacraments as a means of conveying his blessings, albeit in softer language than Calvin would normally have used.

Hence, the accord describes the sacrament both as a sign or seal in Zwinglian fashion and, as Calvin stressed, as an instrument imparting spiritual gifts to believers. In the end, the Zürich Agreement was "good disagreement" at its best among reformed theologians. Yet, like the Wittenberg Concord, this latest Protestant attempt at consensus building inevitably led once again to greater "bad disagreement" with the other side. Many conservative German Protestants reacted violently to this rejection of Luther by the Swiss evangelicals, leading to the development of enduring separate confessional identities for Lutherans and the Reformed.

Catholic and Protestant dialogues

Tyndale and Frith had argued that separating dogma from ceremonies permitted transubstantiation to be considered an "indifferent thing", thus opening a potential way for reconciliation between traditionalists and reformers. Each of these elements – doctrine, ceremonies, and the concept of *adiaphora* – would be important to attempts at church unity in the 1540s. Once again, Bucer led the way, but Melanchthon joined him in these efforts.

Having spent the previous decade trying to bring the reformers to agreement, Bucer spent the 1540s trying to bring reconciliation between Roman Catholics and Protestants. Yet, he did so not only as a means for furthering Christian unity but also with the covert purpose of widening the influence of the basic theological principles of the Reformation in traditionalist areas. At an ecumenical colloquy at Regensburg in 1541, he and Melanchthon attempted the same kind of careful doctrinal language negotiations as they had done in Wittenberg. Since both Roman Catholic and Reformation theologians agreed to the necessity of faith in God's promises and good works of love in the Christian life, if not to how these came about, Bucer helped his Roman Catholic counterpart Cardinal Gasparo Contarini find a linguistic formula acceptable to both sides that highlighted these common commitments. An article was drafted that described justification as the result of the imputation of the alien righteousness of Christ by faith which leads to a lesser, secondary personal righteousness through good works done through the aid of divine grace. These doctrinal efforts ran aground, however, when Contarini insisted on transubstantiation and the Protestants rejected the necessity of confession to a priest. After both the papal court and Luther rejected the Regensburg compromise formula on justification, all efforts at Protestant–Roman Catholic reconciliation through carefully worded confessions came to an end. When the long-sought ecumenical council opened in Trent in 1545, its aim would be the establishing of confessional Roman Catholicism, not Christian reunion.

Despite such a significant setback, Bucer was indefatigable. If confessional agreement could not disseminate Reformation thought packaged in Romanist language, his next attempt began with ecclesiastical rites. Archbishop Hermann von Wied, prince-bishop of Cologne, wanted to bring about much needed reforms in his diocese based on the humanist programme of the Bible and early church practice. He invited Bucer, who was once again joined by Melanchthon, to write up a book of proposals which was published in the archbishop's name as *Simple Consideration Concerning the Establishment of a Christian Reformation Founded upon God's Word* (1543). Bucer and Melanchthon's plan was to use the combination of reformed liturgies (including the mass) and gospel sermons (based on justification by faith) to enable participants to experience the presence of Christ and thus allure traditionalists, step by step, to a new way of thinking and living. Naturally, to use worship services as a means of converting the people, they needed to be in the vernacular. In addition, priests were to be permitted to marry. Ultimately, these efforts also came to nought, in this case because of significant opposition by the conservative and politically powerful cathedral canons, coupled with Charles V's brutal military victory that summer over the Duchy of Jülich-Cleves-Berg, upon which the emperor demanded the cessation of the ecclesiastical reforms that had been gradually introduced there. In the end, the prince-bishop was pressured into resigning.

The imperial truces over religion had always had the clause that they would expire as soon as an ecumenical council met to decide the questions. With the advent of the Council of Trent's first decrees in 1546 and Charles V's military superiority, it was only a matter of time until the ultimate expression of "bad disagreement" – war! – broke out in the empire. On 24 April 1547 imperial troops routed the Saxon elector John Frederick's forces. Philip of Hesse soon surrendered, ending Protestant resistance in the empire. The emperor then imposed the Augsburg Interim (1548). Although in theory it, too, sought unity only in essentials, permitting diversity in non-essentials, its understanding of essentials was indisputably Roman: the pope as interpreter of Scripture, obedience to bishops, transubstantiation, mass as a sacrifice, works-righteousness, and invocation of saints. The Interim's provisional permission for married clergy and lay reception of the cup in the mass brought little comfort to Protestants.

Bucer left for exile in England, though Melanchthon stayed in Wittenberg. As a Lutheran himself, the new Saxon elector had no intention of accepting the Interim, and thus sought some form of compromise between the emperor and his Lutheran subjects. Eventually, Melanchthon agreed to support a modified version called the Leipzig Interim for which he penned a new article upholding justification by faith but which accepted several of the other Roman provisions. In the face of possible further military action by Charles, Melanchthon defended his actions on the grounds that it was the least worst possibility for the conquered Protestants in Saxony. Similar to the arguments put forth by Tyndale and Frith in the previous decade, Melanchthon insisted that it maintained the essentials of the Reformation, particularly the key doctrine of justification by faith, while the traditionalist ceremonies were *adiaphora* which could be conceded. Conservative Lutherans led by Matthias Flacius would brook no such compromise. He attacked Melanchthon bitterly as a traitor to true Lutheranism, for rites reinforced doctrines. In particular, when ceremonies were imposed as something necessary, they ceased to be neutral. As a result, nothing imposed in times of suppression and persecution could be considered indifferent. Siding with Flacius on this point, Lutherans finally settled the dispute in the Formula of Concord (1580).

Archbishop Cranmer and a unifying worship service

When faced with the return of the Latin mass with the accession of Queen Mary of England in 1553, Thomas Cranmer, the Archbishop of Canterbury under Henry VIII and Edward VI, refused to have anything to do with what he considered Satan's blasphemies. As Nicholas Ridley argued, once the Reformation had come to a land, the people could not relapse into their old sins. However, when working towards reform it was a slow and incremental process. During Henry's rule, Cranmer and the other English reformers had lived with traditionalist Latin rites designed to reinforce medieval teachings, even as they worked to change the Church of England's official doctrine. The religious negotiations between England and Germany during Henry's flirtation with joining the Protestant Schmalkadic League in the 1530s had given them their best opportunity to do so. Emerging from the initial round of these discussions, the Bishops' Book (1537) became an interesting example of "good disagreement", for both traditionalists and reformers made sure that their fundamental theological tenets were included, albeit somewhat confusingly side by side. For example, confession to a priest remained necessary for salvation, but the process was redefined to become the forum for preaching the Lutheran understanding of justification by faith to sinners, yet good works were still required as well. As a result, both sides could stress the passages they preferred and ignore others. In the end, however, even the foreign policy benefits of League membership could not induce Henry either to approve explicit Protestant doctrine or to reform traditionalist practices that most offended the Germans, like maintaining transubstantiation, the sacrifice of the mass, clerical celibacy, and the withholding of the chalice from the laity. He clearly codified his theological stance in the Act of Six Articles (1539) and the consistently Erasmian King's Book (1543) which replaced the Bishops' Book.

Under King Edward, however, Cranmer was free to implement a full programme for reform. Following Bucer's approach in the aborted Cologne Reformation, Cranmer decided to use worship services as the means for converting the English people to Protestant principles. As envisioned in *Simple Consideration*, Cranmer combined gospel preaching based on justification by faith with reformed, vernacular liturgies, but he implemented the programme gradually. As he had under Henry, Cranmer began with doctrine. His first liturgical change was to insert mandatory Protestant preaching of the way of salvation into the Latin mass through the required use of the *Book of Homilies* (July 1547). Since these sermons were intended "clearly to put away all contention which hath heretofore risen through diversity of preaching", Cranmer, like Tyndale and Frith before him, was following Bucer in making the right understanding of faith and love the essentials necessary for Christian unity, albeit on a clearly Reformation basis. During the next eight months Cranmer then focused on a steady stream of changes in liturgical practice, which culminated in a new English ending for the Latin mass that banned elevating the consecrated bread and encouraged reception of both the wine and the bread (March 1548). All discussion of Christ's presence was also banned until further notice, in effect making even transubstantiation for the time being an "indifferent thing", as Tyndale and Frith had suggested.

Cranmer believed in the power of Scripture to stir up saving faith and love in the hearts of the people. Consequently, his chief aim in liturgical matters was furthering the gospel through Bible reading and biblically faithful prayers. Yet, as a humanist, Cranmer also understood that any message had to be tailored to its audience. Hence, on the one hand, he argued that religious rites should not be static, because to be effective in proclaiming the gospel to each generation they had to be adapted to ever-evolving national cultures and languages. On the other hand, he insisted that priority should be given to retaining ancient practices, if they could still further the faith of the current generation. Thus, a little over a year later Cranmer introduced the first English prayer book, which institutionalized the systematic reading of Scripture on a twice-daily basis. Moreover, all references to works-righteousness were removed, and Holy Communion emphasized only a sacrifice of praise and thanksgiving, although outwardly it could still be celebrated so as to look like the old mass (June 1549).

While Cranmer had explicitly sought a unifying path between too little and too much reformation, once again "bad disagreement" followed. On the traditionalist end, 7,000 people rose up in rebellion in south-west England against the newfangled prayer book. For Cranmer, ceremonies not contrary to the gospel were *adiaphora* in themselves. But once they had been instituted by lawful government, breaking them was a grave offence against good order in the church and society. As a result, the state responded ruthlessly. Four thousand people were executed after the rebellion, a massive number of deaths – the equivalent of roughly 200,000 people for the current United Kingdom population.

Among the reformers, arguments broke out over whether liturgical ceremonies were, in fact, *adiaphora*, especially if they could be construed by the people as supporting papist errors. These concerns came to a head during the debates over prayer book revision. In keeping with his gradualist approach, Cranmer had intended all along to revise his first prayer book, but the question remained as to how much more revision was needed. The outward appearance of the old mass had to go, but what else? In 1550 he published *A Defence of the True and Catholic Doctrine of the Sacrament of the Body and Blood of our Saviour Christ*, which clearly disavowed transubstantiation and promoted instead a spiritual presence position akin to Calvin and Bullinger's Zürich Agreement, where communicants grew in mutual indwelling with Christ through faith. Cranmer had offered England as a refuge to many continental theologians, including Bucer, Peter Martyr Vermigli, and Jan Laski. With so many top Protestant theologians already residing in England, Cranmer also tried unsuccessfully to induce Melanchthon and Calvin to come and join them for a Protestant general council as the best response to the Roman council at Trent. Naturally, the hottest theological topic for such an attempt at Protestant unity remained the Lord's Supper, and for the Reformation theologians resident in England, how best to express that doctrine in the next English prayer book.

Jan Laski argued powerfully for a mere memorialist position. However, influenced by Bucer's written suggestions (as a recently identified prayer book from the revision committee makes clear), the final version of the 1552 prayer book kept the Calvinist side of the Zürich Agreement. Although communicants were told to "Take and eat this in remembrance that Christ died for you" (suggesting a memorial meal), a crucial phrase was restored after being initially deleted: "that we may evermore dwell in him and he in us" (suggesting spiritual impartation of Christ as well). Yet, even after the doctrinal wording had been carefully decided, at the very last minute, after the actual printing had begun, the divisive issue of ceremonies on this most sensitive topic reared its ugly head. Appealing to the king's council, John Knox strenuously opposed the retention of kneeling for receiving Holy Communion. Rejecting Cranmer's definition of *adiaphora* as those things neither required nor contrary to the gospel, he insisted "Whatsoever is not commanded in the scripture, is against the scripture and utterly unlawful and ungodly." Since kneeling was an unscriptural tradition implying adoration, he demanded that communicants sit instead. While Cranmer agreed that faith and morals had to be based on the clear command of Scripture, he utterly rejected as far too narrow Knox's argument that everything else in life had to follow a biblical rule as well.[9] Rites and ceremonies, as particular expressions of the gospel for different eras and cultures, were derived from the institutional authority of the church. As long as they did not contradict biblical truth, the church could draw on other sources like the ancient traditions of monasticism or institute new forms of prayer more in keeping with contemporary needs, even if such practices were not explicitly detailed in Scripture. Cranmer's distinction lies behind that famous Anglican dictum in Article 6 of the Thirty-Nine Articles: "Holy Scripture contains all things necessary for salvation." The Bible plainly teaches everything Christians need to know about faith and morals; no other source is needed for saving knowledge. However, how these truths are to be institutionalized in the life of the church and proclaimed to the surrounding culture is the responsibility of church leaders to discern and devise.

Cranmer won the argument with the council by the donnish quip that if Knox really wanted the Church of England to receive Communion in the biblical manner, they would need to recline on the ground in the chancel rather than sit at a table. While seeming perhaps merely a witty retort *ad absurdum,* Cranmer was actually pointing out that there was no such thing as only one "biblical" way to eat food. The manner of one's eating was a thing indifferent determined by one's culture. In the end, the 1552 prayer book retained kneeling to receive Communion, and Knox had to be content with the last-minute "Black Rubric", which specifically denied a Roman interpretation of the practice. The following year Cranmer sealed his victory by including his understanding of ceremonies in what would become Article 34 of the Thirty-Nine Articles:

It is not necessary that traditions and ceremonies be in all places one, or utterly like. For at all times they have been diverse, and may be changed, according to the diversity of countries, and men's manners, so that nothing be ordained against God's Word.

Conclusion

Throughout the sixteenth century, unity in the essentials was seen as the great hope for church renewal. The difficulty was in deciding what those essentials were. Since Erasmus's humanism looked to the Bible primarily for moral instruction, his essentials of salvation stressed the freedom of the human will to choose to fulfil the teachings of Christ with God's help. Since Luther looked to the teachings of Paul on salvation, his gospel essentials began with what Christ had accomplished on the cross and then had freely given to a helpless humanity through the gift of faith. Despite sincere attempts, the gulf between these two fundamentally different understandings of salvation was unbridgeable. In the end, both sides decided that ultimately saving truth was more important than even institutional unity. Thus, Western Christianity became divided between Roman Catholics and Protestants.

Yet, even among those who shared Luther's commitment to justification by faith alone through grace alone, essential differences also arose. Nevertheless, ironically, even these difficult debates helped evangelical groups to clarify their own views, leading ultimately to historic accords which became the basis for future Protestant identities: the Zürich Agreement (Reformed), the Edwardian formularies (Anglican), and the Book of Concord (Lutheran). In turn, the Protestant challenge to traditional Catholicism brought about the Council of Trent, thereby bringing theological consolidation and much needed reform to the Roman Church. Thus, despite its reputation for "bad disagreement", the Reformation era did, in fact, produce important examples of limited "good disagreement". How did these accords come about?

First, despite their significant differences, all sixteenth-century Christians realized that it was a scandal for the church to be divided. All were committed to as much unity as possible, even if that eventually meant the creation of Christian denominations instead of a single unified church.

Second, everyone recognized that theological truth mattered, and thus was worth the considerable time, study, and trouble involved in discussing the issues as thoroughly as possible to see what common ground could be found with others. For all the major agreements, this search required years of debate, draft proposals, periods of disappointing disagreement, and, most importantly, patient persistence before an enduring agreement could be reached.

Third, everyone recognized that not all theological issues were of equal importance. The difficulty was in deciding the basis for ranking them. In the end, the unity that was achieved among Protestants came about because: (1) there was basic agreement about the source of authority for determining faith and practice – the Bible; (2) each side came to respect and value what was most important to the other; and (3) each side was willing to consider that some of their views were of secondary importance and could be left out of the discussion for the sake of unity.

Fourth, personal relationships were the key to progress. Mutual trust had to be established among the leaders for each side to begin to learn what really mattered to the other and why. Only when participants could understand and respect the primary theological principle that motivated the people across the table could they agree to set aside some of their own concerns.

As for "good disagreement" in England, characteristically Archbishop Cranmer combined several of the approaches we have seen in this period. He chose to found his Christian essentials on an overtly Protestant understanding of Scripture and the way of salvation, emphasizing scriptural self-interpretation, saving faith, grateful love, and their fruit of a godly life. He then required the clear and unambiguous preaching of these essentials in every parish church, although he was willingly to live with the Latin mass as well for two years to give people time to adjust. When he reformed the mass, he declared that ceremonies were *adiaphora*, as long as they did not conflict with Scripture, enabling him to give priority to retaining ancient practices to allure people to the gospel through them. When he described Christ's eucharistic presence, he followed the example of the carefully worded Zürich Agreement by using both instrumentalist and memorialist language in his second prayer book. Lastly, when it was clear that there would be no general Protestant council, he drew up articles of religion which enshrined in the Church of England the distinction between Scripture as the sole basis for unity in the essentials of faith and morals (with no one passage interpreted so as to contradict another), and Scripture as providing wide parameters for the development of institutional life in both the church and wider culture. Thus, Cranmer gave future generations of English-speaking Christians generous room for both human creativity and "good disagreement" in the pursuit of God and a better society.

***

Questions

1. How does knowledge of church history give us fresh perspectives on our own struggles and successes today?

2. In what ways do the historic disagreements of the Reformation still shape church life in your local context?

3. To what extent do disagreements about the authority of Scripture underpin other disagreements between Christians today?

4. In the Reformation political differences combined with theological differences in dividing Christians. How does theology get intertwined

with political, social, and cultural differences today? How should we react when this happens?

5. What lessons can we learn from how the leading reformers sought to overcome their disagreements?

6

Ecumenical (Dis)agreements

Andrew Atherstone and Martin Davie

In the light of Jesus' prayer for unity, this chapter explores the different ways Christian ecumenism has sought to overcome the historic disagreements which have divided the church into multiple denominations. It sets out various informal approaches to making Christian unity visible, and the goals of formal inter-church dialogues which pursue "organic unity" or "reconciled diversity". The chapter explains the need for ecumenical conversations to face disagreements openly and to identify the Christian fundamentals, and highlights the importance of this work for the church's mission today.

The ecumenical challenge

Jesus' famous prayer for the Christian church on the night of his arrest has become the touchstone of the ecumenical movement. John's Gospel records:

> *I do not pray for these only [the apostles], but also for those who believe in me through their word, that they may all be one, even as you, Father, are in me, and I in you, that they also may be in us, so that the world may believe that you have sent me. The glory that you have given me I have given to them, that they may be one even as we are one, I in them and you in me, that they may become perfectly one, so that the world may know that you have sent me and loved them even as you loved me. (John 17:20–23)*

It is a remarkable prayer, establishing an intimate connection between the unity Jesus enjoys with his heavenly Father, and the unity which Christians enjoy together. At one level that prayer is answered by the unseen "unity in the Spirit" (Ephesians 4:3) which binds Jesus' global family together, and in the unity anticipated in the next life among the glorious company of heaven (Revelation 7:9). But Jesus prays specifically that the unity of his disciples would be a public testimony to a watching world. E.J. Poole-Connor, founder of the Fellowship of Independent Evangelical Churches (FIEC), comments:

> *His prayer that their unity might induce the world to believe that the Father had sent Him could be fulfilled only by its external manifestation. The world has no faculty of faith to behold the invisible. The saint believes in order to see; our Lord prayed that the world might see in order to believe.*

Therefore it will not do to "close our eyes to the wreckage of the visible church and dreamily to murmur that all is well". Poole-Connor continues: "Aloofness, exclusiveness, schism – these things are as alien to our Lord's ideal for His Church as darkness is from light. It was, moreover, to be a unity which should compel the world to believe; in other words, a unity so palpable as to be visible even to the purblind."[1]

But the reality is far different. Indeed, one of the facts most obvious about the Christian church worldwide is its multiple divisions. Some estimates put the total number of Christian denominations at over 30,000.[2] And every local community illustrates these institutional divisions in bricks and mortar – separate church buildings, often on the same street, from different denominations with distinct identities, confessions, and liturgies. Even if they now live notionally at peace, friends instead of rivals, their visible separation is proof that the historic disagreements run deep. The two villages in which we as authors live, in Kent and Oxfordshire, are a case in point. Meopham, near Gravesend, has four separate churches: the medieval parish church (previously, of course, Roman Catholic until the Reformation); a Strict Baptist chapel built in the 1820s; a second Baptist congregation established in the 1920s when some left the Strict Baptists because of their "closed" communion policy; and a Roman Catholic church consecrated in the 1960s. Eynsham, near Oxford, likewise has a medieval parish church, built by the pre-Reformation Benedictine abbey; a Hanoverian Baptist chapel; a Roman Catholic church, originally established in the 1890s as a mission which met in a private house; a Methodist chapel (now colonized by the Anglicans for a church hall); and a Catholic Apostolic church (now converted into housing).

These stories could be multiplied across the country. Eastern Orthodox, Congregational, United Reformed, Brethren, Moravian, Mennonite, Pentecostal, Free Evangelical, Quaker, Salvation Army, to name but a few – separated denominations reflecting Christianity's divided history. Sometimes the original reasons for their separation are long since forgotten; sometimes they are painfully fresh, the result of recent hostilities. But the world looks on in bewilderment. Far from being a witness to the glories of the gospel and the majesty of Jesus Christ, the church's public disagreements are a scandal and a confusion. If a united church attracts people to the Christian message, a divided church does the opposite. It becomes a laughing-stock and even an object of revulsion. In the face of these facts, what does genuine church unity look like? Given the existence of multiple Christian traditions, can our disagreements be overcome?

Making unity visible

There are numerous ways in which Christians manifest unity which transcends denominational boundaries. At its most fundamental level, this is evident among Christians who are deliberately and joyfully disinterested in historic disagreements, which seem like the irrelevant clanging of ancient battles. Many choose their local church not because of its denomination, or its doctrinal basis, but because of the quality of preaching or music or youth work, or because of its friendship and welcome. For many it is simply the fact that it is their *local* church, perhaps the only one in the community. In England, Anglican congregations in particular often include many who by inclination or upbringing are really Baptists or Methodists and still identify as such. But these denominational disagreements have little impact at the grass-roots level, and as a result "ecumenism" is relegated to the business of theologians and synods. In fact, of course, these local Christians are putting ecumenism into practice every day.

There is a considerable amount of what we might call "accidental ecumenism", the free interflow of theological ideas and resources across all traditions. Christian hymnody is particularly adaptable, with hymns from the likes of Isaac Watts, Charles Wesley, John Henry Newman, and Timothy Dudley-Smith sung throughout the English-speaking world, despite their contrasting Dissenting, Methodist, Roman Catholic, and Anglican affiliations. New songwriters are often hard to place denominationally, although many have recently emerged from the Vineyard and Hillsong networks, bringing Californian and Australian brands to a global market. Christian conventions and festivals, such as Greenbelt, Keswick, Soul Survivor, and Word Alive, draw people together out of the comfort zones of their familiar churches. The best-selling Christian literature likewise reaches into many diverse congregations. Evangelistic programmes, like the Alpha course, have also been hugely significant in bridging denominational divides. Although launched within the charismatic wing of Anglicanism, Alpha has reached across the world into almost every ecclesial context.

Informal ecumenism has been pioneered in other ways too. For example, one reaction against the deep divisions of the Second World War was the ecumenical monastic community established at Taizé in France in the 1940s by Brother Roger Schütz, a Swiss Protestant. It has since grown into a vibrant multilingual, interdenominational Christian community, a place of pilgrimage for tens of thousands of young people every year. Taizé embraces cultural diversity and a multitude of Christian styles, but divisions over doctrine and church order are left at the door.[3] Chemin Neuf (New Way) is another ecumenical religious order with roots in France, founded in Lyon in 1973 by Laurent Fabre, a young Jesuit who had experienced charismatic renewal. It now has over 1,200 members in 26 countries and nearly 10,000 associate members. Its theological emphases are simplicity of life, Ignatian spirituality, "baptism in the Holy Spirit", mission, and Christian unity. It was the first to run the Alpha course among Roman Catholics in France.

The emergence of the charismatic movement has been particularly influential in blurring denominational boundaries. Former Archbishop of Canterbury George Carey recalls how in the 1970s he was forced to take seriously the ecumenical claim that "God is working through his Spirit in all the traditions" when an Anglo-Catholic friend, John Gunstone, prayed for him in "tongues".[4] He argues that a primary task of the Holy Spirit is "making the disparate into one",[5] and in his ecumenical treatise *The Meeting of the Waters* (1985) he describes the charismatic movement as

> *the only revival in history which has united evangelicals on the one hand, with their strong emphasis on the death of Christ and full atonement, and Roman Catholics on the other, with their emphasis on the sacraments. Somehow charismatic experiences have brought together people who on the face of it have little in common theologically.*

As evidence of this Carey recommends attending a renewal meeting:

> *you will observe that church affiliation is put quietly aside as Christians worship their common Lord: Catholics, Protestants and Orthodox, all finding that the ground before the cross is level and that the Spirit does not dispense his gifts according to our ecclesiastical pedigree.*

Furthermore, he notes that without the Holy Spirit "unity schemes may resemble the marriage of corpses".[6]

At a formal level, in conversations between ministers and denominations, historic disagreements and doctrinal divisions necessarily come into focus. To what extent can congregations work together despite these disagreements? Francis Schaeffer, Christian apologist and founder of L'Abri in Switzerland, developed the idea of "co-belligerence" – that churches can go into battle together on specific issues of social concern, without the need for doctrinal agreement. Such joint action might include food banks, shelters for the homeless, debt counselling services, or campaigns on issues such as people trafficking, climate change, global debt, and in defence of the persecuted church.

A greater level of core agreement about the gospel message is necessary if local congregations are to extend their cooperation from co-belligerence to co-mission, such as combined youth work or joint evangelistic campaigns. It makes little sense for churches to preach together if they are not happy to pray together, or if they disagree over who should "follow up" new believers. Nevertheless, because unity and mission are so closely interwoven, a corporate witness can be especially fruitful. Billy Graham began his ministry as a fundamentalist preacher in the 1940s, working exclusively with like-minded evangelicals, but soon he changed his policy and agreed to combine efforts with Christians of all theological streams in order to promote the gospel. In the words of Mark Noll, he successfully "traded angularity for access".[7] Graham explained: "My own position was that we should be willing to work with all who were willing to work with us."[8] He habitually shared a platform with Roman Catholic cardinals and archbishops, especially during city-wide crusades. "I feel that I belong to all the churches," he told David Frost.[9] Other globally renowned evangelists, like the Argentinians Luis Palau and Ed Silvoso, have a similar ecumenical emphasis.

If inter-church disagreements can be temporarily overlooked for the sake of co-belligerence and co-mission, they must be addressed head-on when formal union or merger is anticipated. Most towns have an informal Churches Together network, fostering friendly collaboration between churches, but some have gone a step further and entered a covenant relationship while keeping their separate identities. Elsewhere denominations have joined forces to create Local Ecumenical Partnerships (LEPs) where knotty questions over faith and order must be hammered out: What doctrine will be preached? What liturgy and sacraments? Who appoints the ministers? Who makes the decisions? Although it is possible to live with differences of opinion and even some variety of practice, these disagreements must be resolved sooner or later if the congregation is to flourish.

Ecumenical dialogues

A willingness to talk is an essential prerequisite to overcoming church divisions, but much hinges on whether the conversation partners recognize each other as true churches. If not, ecumenical dialogue becomes interfaith dialogue and the possibility of Christian unity is ruled out, *tout court*, before the conversations begin. As the spirit of *aggiornamento* swept through the Roman Catholic Church, the Second Vatican Council's decree on ecumenism, *Unitatis Redintegratio* (1964), recognized Christians outside the Roman fold as "separated brethren". This opened a door to new ecumenical possibilities. Likewise a major shift in evangelical relations with Rome was indicated by the affirmation of the second National Evangelical Anglican Congress at Nottingham in 1977: "Seeing ourselves and Roman Catholics as fellow Christians, we repent of attitudes that have seemed to deny it."[10] Ecumenical dialogue presupposes difference but also some core agreement.

Much ecumenical discussion takes place informally. Sometimes it is at a personal level, as seen in the liberal–evangelical dialogue about essentials between David Edwards and John Stott, who though both Anglicans came from starkly different theological perspectives.[11] Often groups of theologians engage in structured conversations, but without official sponsorship from their denominations. For example, in the 1920s the Malines Conversations (at Malines, or Mechelen, near Antwerp) brought Anglo-Catholics and Roman Catholics together for groundbreaking discussions, at the initiative of Lord Halifax (a leading Anglo-Catholic layman) and Cardinal Mercier (a Belgian archbishop). Their proceedings were initially top secret and came to an end when the papal encyclical *Mortalium Animos* (1928) condemned the ecumenical movement and reasserted that true unity was found only in submission to the Roman Church.[12] Others picked up the baton, such as the Groupe des Dombes, a private gathering of Catholic and Protestant theologians launched by Abbé Paul Couturier in the 1930s and meeting ever since. In the early 1990s, and with similarly controversial results, the movement Evangelicals and Catholics Together (ECT) initiated conversations in the United States between representative leaders, including Charles Colson, Avery Dulles, Richard John Neuhaus, and John White. The ECT statement expressed their common convictions on Christian faith and mission, and was described as "an invitation to reexamine stereotypes, prejudices, and conventional ideas that have been entrenched, in some cases, for almost five hundred years". They acknowledged that ECT was merely "a beginning", but announced: "a conversation has been started, and that conversation bears the promise of multiplying the power of gospel proclamation to a world increasingly threatened by a culture of decadence and death".[13]

Formal ecumenical dialogues, between official denominational representatives, are multitudinous but often lack the energy and creativity of informal conversations and can drag on for years. The Anglican–Roman Catholic International Commission (ARCIC), meeting since 1970, has published reports on eucharistic doctrine, ordination, authority, salvation and the church, life in Christ, and the Virgin Mary, as well as further "elucidations" and "clarifications" of earlier statements.[14] The international Lutheran–Reformed Dialogue, between the Lutheran World Federation and the World Alliance of Reformed Churches, has tackled the topics of predestination, Christology, the Lord's Supper, and the nature of the church. A vast number of other examples could be named. The purpose of such conversations is not only to seek agreement, but also to bring areas of disagreement into sharper focus in order to clarify the real sticking points. Jesuit theologian Francis Clark writes:

> *In the long run the ecumenical cause will be better served by frank scrutiny of the roots of disagreement than by ignoring them. The clear-sighted candour of writers… who are able to recognize the incompatibility of two doctrinal positions and to point out the reason, is more useful than the well-meant but undiscerning eirenism of writers who treat contradictory doctrines as complementary insights, as different emphases of the same truth, as different colours in one spectrum of Christian witness.[15]*

The result of honest conversations between divided churches may be that different positions are shown to be incompatible and contradictory, and therefore the divisions must remain. This does not make the conversations fruitless but, on the contrary, pinpoints where change is necessary for unity to proceed. J.I. Packer laments that in some ecumenical circles *confession* and *confessionalism* are "dirty words", and warns against "the pathological state sometimes called 'ecumania' – the uncontrolled urge to merge", which short-circuits serious discussion.[16] Likewise Philip Edgcumbe Hughes censures

> *the undiscerning attitude of mind which sees all and sundry through rose-tinted spectacles, which deprecates theology as divisive, and encourages dialogue in which accommodation is found for all points of view… But goodwill without discernment is a corrosive that eats away the foundations of the Church of Christ. The distinctives of the Christian faith cannot be bartered for the blandishments of a fashionable bonhomie.[17]*

The purpose of proper ecumenical conversation is precisely to remove those rose-tinted spectacles. Sometimes when disagreements and divisions are probed deeply, they are shown to be highly significant; but others may be revealed as entirely insubstantial and easily overcome. The need to disentangle theology from personality and past history is particularly acute. From a Scottish perspective, Donald Macleod observes:

> *in many instances, it would be hypocrisy to claim that our divisions had anything to do with doctrinal considerations at all. Many of them have been the result of differences of opinion on matters of Church government, worship and discipline: of disputes on baptism, exclusive psalmody, and relations with the state. Too many churches are split-offs from other churches and owe their existence to nothing more honourable than clashes of personality.*[18]

In fact, Macleod suggests, as far as doctrine is concerned there is a surprising amount of unanimity among Christians across the globe.

Ecumenical goals

What is the ultimate goal of ecumenism? What is the best model of church unity to aim for in the long term? Some argue for "organic unity" – that is, one worldwide church, visibly united, with an agreed pattern of doctrine and order, though perhaps allowing for variety of worship styles in different cultural contexts. Anything less than this visible unity, they suggest, testifies to a divided body of Christ and falls short of God's desire for his people. In the aftermath of the First World War, which had seen the leading industrialized nations blast each other to smithereens in the trenches, the churches took a lead in calling for reconciliation. But unity begins at home, so the 1920 Lambeth Conference of Anglican bishops issued an "Appeal to All Christian People", inviting them to seek a reunited church. In remarkably militaristic language, it declared:

The Faith cannot be adequately apprehended and the battle of the Kingdom cannot be worthily fought while the body is divided, and is thus unable to grow up into the fullness of the life of Christ. The time has come, we believe, for all the separated groups of Christians to agree in forgetting the things which are behind and reaching out towards the goal of a reunited Catholic Church. The removal of the barriers which have arisen between them will only be brought about by a new comradeship of those whose faces are definitely set in this way.

The vision which rises before us is that of a Church, genuinely Catholic, loyal to all Truth, and gathering into its fellowship all "who profess and call themselves Christians," within whose visible unity all the treasures of faith and order, bequeathed as a heritage by the past to the present, shall be possessed in common, and made serviceable to the whole Body of Christ. Within this unity Christian Communions now separated from one another would retain much that has long been distinctive in their methods of worship and service. It is through a rich diversity of life and devotion that the unity of the whole fellowship will be fulfilled.[19]

Here was a classic call for "unity in diversity", in which all professing Christians would be visibly united in one church. The Lambeth Appeal was a catalyst for major ecumenical conversations during the 1920s and 1930s.

The bitter violence of the Second World War generated a similar longing for peace and reconciliation, not just in theory but in visible practice. The World Council of Churches (WCC), launched in 1948, set itself the goal of reuniting separated denominations in one global, institutional church. At its third assembly in New Delhi in 1961 it acknowledged that perfect unity "will be known in its fullness only when all things are consummated by Christ in his glory", but also that it was a divine imperative "to seek the unity which he wills for his Church *on earth here and now*". So the goal of ecumenism was not just the eschatological hope of reconciliation in heaven; it could be made manifest in our world today. The New Delhi report continued:

> *We believe that the unity which is both God's will and his gift to his Church is being made visible as all in each place who are baptized into Jesus Christ and confess him as Lord and Saviour are brought by the Holy Spirit into one fully committed fellowship, holding the one apostolic faith, preaching the one Gospel, breaking the one bread, joining in common prayer, and having a corporate life reaching out in witness and service to all and who at the same time are united with the whole Christian fellowship in all places and all ages in such wise that ministry and members are accepted by all, and that all can act and speak together as occasion requires for the tasks to which God calls his people. It is for such unity that we believe we must pray and work.[20]*

This statement deliberately echoes the language of the Book of Acts with its beautiful portrait of the early Christian believers who were devoted to the apostles' teaching and fellowship, to the breaking of bread and to prayer, and who held all things in common (Acts 2:42). By implication, the New Testament model of unity is not a rosy picture of some halcyon Christian past, but should be the realistic desire and goal of the church today. The New Delhi report was clear that unity must be made "visible" and its most famous phrase, "*all in each place*", implies one local church in each community to which all Christians belong.

Organic unity can be reached in two directions – from the top down, at one swift stroke, with formal agreement between entire denominations at synodical level – or from the bottom up, slowly and incrementally, beginning with grass-roots unity between local congregations. The second approach was famously argued in *Growing into Union* (1970), a controversial ecumenical treatise written by a quartet of Anglican theologians. They proposed that decisions on union should be taken at a local level, not imposed as a blanket rule by the ecclesiastical hierarchy, which often made congregations feel like "pawns in someone else's game". Whereas many official unity schemes imposed uniformity of church order but allowed disagreements over doctrine, *Growing into Union* advocated the opposite – that where there was doctrinal consensus between local groups of Christians about the essentials of the gospel, then "temporary anomalies of a pluriform practice" should be accepted while "on the road to union". In other words, it was a case of "doing what you can where you can", and letting the rest of the denomination catch up later.[21]

During the mid-twentieth century there were several successful experiments in organic unity, by which separated denominations sacrificed their own independence to form united churches.[22] The Church of South India, launched in 1947, was especially significant as a merger of episcopal and non-episcopal ministries, encompassing Anglicans, Methodists, Presbyterians, and Congregationalists. It took as its motto Jesus' words "That They All May Be One" (John 17:21). In Britain, a number of old fractures were healed. Scottish Presbyterianism had witnessed multiple divisions since the "Disruption" of 1843 – including the "Wee Frees" and the "Wee Wee Frees" – but in 1929 there was some modest reunion when the bulk of the United Free Church of Scotland reintegrated with the Church of Scotland. Methodism had also experienced numerous splits, but in 1932 the Wesleyan Methodists, Primitive Methodists, and United Methodists were reunited. Two generations later, in 1972, Presbyterians and Congregationalists came together in the United Reformed Church (URC), later joined by the Association of the Churches of Christ, despite their disagreements over ecclesiology. Anglicans and Methodists also debated formal organic union, but fell short at the final hurdle. On a wave of ebullient ecumenical optimism, the first British Conference on Faith and Order at Nottingham in 1964 agreed to seek the unity of all British churches by Easter Sunday 1980. With the benefit of hindsight such a naïve hope seems wildly unrealistic, even rather silly. Mark Chapman has described the ecumenical dreams of the nineteenth century, especially between the Church of England and the Roman Catholic Church, as "the fantasy of reunion".[23] There was plenty of fantasy in the twentieth century too.

The dilemma for ecumenism is that each time a fracture is healed, another fracture appears in a different place. So, for example, during the church mergers of the twentieth century there were always some who refused to join the new body (whether for doctrinal or personal reasons) and remained behind as a separated rump. Even when the bulk of Christians join together, the number of denominations is seldom reduced. New friendships often lead to the cooling of old friendships. When Anglican evangelicals made a deliberate decision at the Keele Congress in 1967 to start building bridges with non-evangelical Anglicans, they inevitably found themselves drifting away from non-Anglican evangelicals.[24] Paradoxically, therefore, ecumenism can result in healed relationships and broken relationships at the same time.

An alternative ambition, rather than full "organic unity", is "reconciled diversity". A good example is the Community of Protestant Churches in Europe (CPCE), which numbers over ninety Lutheran and Reformed churches from over thirty countries and includes two pre-Reformation networks, the Waldensians and the Czech Brethren. Together they claim to represent approximately 50 million Protestants. These churches were divided at the Reformation by deep theological disagreements and competing confessional statements, but now subscribe to the 1973 Leuenberg Agreement, which attempts to overcome the institutional hostilities between Protestants which are a legacy of the sixteenth century.[25] The Agreement declares:

> In the course of four centuries, the theological grappling with the questions of modernity, the development of biblical research, the church renewal movements and the rediscovery of an ecumenical perspective have led the churches of the Reformation in similar directions to new ways of thinking and living. Admittedly, these developments have also given rise to new differences which cut across the confessions. But again and again, especially in times of common suffering, there has been an experience of Christian fellowship. All this led the churches, especially

since the revival movements, to seek to give contemporary expression
to the biblical witness and the Reformation confessions of faith. In
this way they have learned to distinguish between the fundamental
witness of the Reformation confessions of faith and their historically
conditioned thought forms.

It goes on to explain that conflicting views over the Lord's Supper, Christology, and predestination, which historically separated Lutheran and Reformed, are no longer a bar to fellowship, because consensus is possible. In line with the reformers, it argues that "the necessary and sufficient pre-requisite for the true unity of the Church is agreement in the right teaching of the Gospel and the right administration of the sacraments". That gospel is encapsulated by the Leuenberg Agreement as justification by faith in Jesus Christ, "the message of God's free grace". On that basis the churches of the CPCE extend "pulpit and table fellowship" to each other, and the mutual recognition of baptism and ordination. It is reconciled diversity, with major implications for interdenominational friendship and corporate witness, but not full unification. The churches remain independent, with their separate confessions and doctrinal distinctions, and admit:

There remain considerable differences between our churches in forms
of worship, types of spirituality, and church order. These differences
are often more deeply felt in the congregations than the traditional
doctrinal differences. Nevertheless, in fidelity to the New Testament and
Reformation criteria for church fellowship, we cannot discern in these
differences any factors which should divide the church.

The CPCE's report, *The Church of Jesus Christ* (1995), likewise reiterates the need for consensus on justification by grace alone, and states: "Where this criterion is satisfied church fellowship as fellowship in word and sacrament can be declared and practised."[26] Nevertheless there is continuing debate among the churches belonging to the

CPCE about how much diversity in faith and practice is truly compatible with this central tenet of justification.

Seeking the fundamentals

When the WCC was established in 1948 its basis, as written into its constitution, was deliberately minimal: "The World Council of Churches is a fellowship of churches which accept our Lord Jesus Christ as God and Saviour." This statement was explicitly Christological and echoed the very brief summary of the gospel given by the apostle Paul, "If you declare with your mouth, 'Jesus is Lord', and believe in your heart that God raised him from the dead, you will be saved" (Romans 10:9; NIV). The WCC basis was strengthened in 1961 to include reference to the Bible and the Trinity, and now reads as follows:

> *The World Council of Churches is a fellowship of churches which confess the Lord Jesus Christ as God and Saviour according to the Scriptures, and therefore seek to fulfil together their common calling to the glory of the one God, Father, Son and Holy Spirit.*

Although it now used the word "confess", the WCC central committee made clear that this basis was not intended as a full creedal statement, but merely "to say what holds us together in the World Council, what is the starting-point of our conversation and the foundation of our collaboration".[27] Nevertheless, it was widely criticized for not saying more about the substance of the Christian message or indeed about the person and work of Jesus Christ. The phrase "according to the Scriptures" echoes Paul's language in 1 Corinthians 15:1–5, but without his doctrinal content concerning the death and resurrection of Jesus.

Among the critics of the WCC was John Stott, who complained that:

*This "lowest common denominator" approach gives the impression...
of a regrettable indifference to revealed truth. It has also led sometimes
to a love of the ambiguous statement which conceals deep and sincerely
held differences and does no lasting good. It merely papers over
the cracks. This looks nice and tidy for a while, for the cracks are
temporarily hidden from view. They remain there beneath the surface,
however, and will one day break into sight again, by that time probably
wider and deeper than before. It is neither honest nor helpful to make
out that divergent opinions are in reality different ways of saying the
same thing.*

Stott argues that public displays of church unity can sometimes be "a game of let's pretend; it is not living in the real world". He continues: "The proper activity of professing Christians who disagree with one another is neither to ignore, nor to conceal, nor even to minimize differences, but to debate them."[28]

One commentator observes: "As we think of Christian unity it is like standing at a fork in a roadway. Two possibilities are before us: false unity and true unity."[29] False unity neglects the gospel and disguises disagreements in order to promote the unity of the visible church as an institution. True unity seeks to give visible expression to Christian fellowship, rooted in a common obedience to the call of Christ. It is therefore essential for any ecumenical venture to identify the "fundamental doctrines" of the gospel which bind Christians together. Macleod identifies these as:

1. doctrines that are revealed in Scripture with such clarity that all Christians are agreed on them

2. doctrines that Scripture itself describes as fundamental

3. doctrines that the church has sought to define and safeguard in its great creeds.[30]

Some ecumenists have downplayed truth in the search for unity. Some anti-ecumenists have neglected unity in defence of truth. But

Christian unity and Christian truth are not polar opposites – they belong always together and are inextricably linked, as Archbishop Justin Welby explains:

> *Are truth and unity opposites, are they competing, do they fight each other?... You often hear that said, but read the Bible! Jesus reveals the truth and Jesus prays that we may be one. Was Jesus wrong? It must be possible for us to live in truth and unity. That is the will and purpose of Christ.*[31]

If the WCC has a minimal basis of fellowship, other Christians have adopted a maximal approach. The English puritans of the mid-seventeenth century, for instance, scrapped the Thirty-Nine Articles of Religion and replaced them with the much fuller Westminster Confession. Every basis, however long or short, is intended to be both exclusive and inclusive, by laying down boundary-markers for fellowship. The basis of the Evangelical Alliance, for example, insists upon the inspiration and authority of Scripture, the virgin birth, substitutionary atonement, the bodily resurrection of Christ and his personal return, the priesthood of all believers, justification by faith alone, and the reality of judgment and eternal condemnation. But it is also deliberately silent on questions which divide evangelicals such as the sacraments, ordination, spiritual gifts, pre-millennialism, the historicity of Adam and Eve, and the nature of hell. Whether ecumenical statements should be long or short is a matter of debate, but whether maximal or minimal none are fully inclusive, because all agree that the Christian church must have boundaries of some description. Even the WCC, despite its widest embrace, excludes those churches that do not acknowledge the Trinity. The search for Christian unity presupposes that Christians stand for something, which is why the fundamental question at the heart of all ecumenical discussion remains: "What is a Christian?"

If the purpose of an ecumenical statement is not to define a denominational subgroup, but to open a conversation, then it must necessarily begin with areas of consensus (however brief) as a platform for further discussion. The historic Christian creeds, which pre-date many of the divisions in world Christianity, are a popular place to start because they are part of the precious heritage of most denominations. The Lambeth Conference of 1888 proposed a four-point platform, first developed by American theologian William Reed Huntington in *The Church Idea: An Essay Toward Unity* (1870), as a good starting point for ecumenical conversation. The so-called Chicago–Lambeth Quadrilateral can be summarized as follows:

1. the Holy Scriptures of the Old and New Testaments as the rule and ultimate standard of faith

2. the Nicene Creed as the sufficient statement of the Christian faith

3. the two sacraments ordained by Christ himself: baptism and the Lord's Supper

4. the historic episcopate, locally adapted.

This Quadrilateral is deliberately flexible and succinct, and somewhat ambiguous. As with every conversation-opener, the terms deserve to be probed. Roman Catholic dialogue partners want to clarify what is meant by the Holy Scriptures – do they include the Old Testament Apocrypha, as laid down at the Council of Trent? The Eastern Orthodox want to clarify which Nicene Creed is meant – although an ecumenical text, it remains a point of historic division between East and West since at least the Schism of 1054, because the Western church has unilaterally added the word *filioque* to the original ("The Holy Spirit proceeds from the Father *and the Son*"). The Salvation Army and the Society of Friends (the Quakers), who do not have sacraments, want to ask why they should thereby be excluded from the Christian church. Baptists and Presbyterians want to probe what is meant by the "historic episcopate, locally adapted". Does it mean authorized oversight of congregations, or a special order of bishops in tactile succession back to the apostle Peter? When interpreted rigidly, the Chicago–Lambeth Quadrilateral closes down conversation. But as a discussion-starter, it enables Christian disagreements to be brought to the table and thoroughly scrutinized and wrestled over in the long search for visible unity in the gospel.

Ecumenism and mission

In his encyclical letter *Ut Unum Sint* (1995), Pope John Paul II proclaimed: "it is absolutely clear that ecumenism, the movement promoting Christian unity, is not just some sort of 'appendix' which is added to the Church's traditional activity. Rather, ecumenism is an organic part of her life and work, and consequently must pervade all that she is and does."[32] The pope soon followed this with a joint declaration with the Archbishop of Canterbury, appealing for their separated communions to give a united witness wherever possible, "for our divisions obscure the gospel message of reconciliation and hope."[33] As has been seen, the search for Christian reconciliation and visible unity is a missionary imperative. Reconciled churches, united on the Christian fundamentals and able to handle their disagreements in a gracious and godly manner, are more effective in their public witness to a watching world. Conversely, unhealed divisions between Christians are "a terrible wound affecting our evangelism".[34]

George Carey argues that if the gospel is about reconciliation between God and humanity, then the church must be reconciled within itself for this message to be given any credence:

> *The ultimate reconciliation that should concern us all is for the world to be reconciled with its Maker. Thus, ecumenism is about liberating the Church to get on with the task of mission. It is about being a credible instrument, a prophetic sign and an eschatological foretaste of the healing of Christ. So yes, it does matter that Churches are in unreconciled diversity because how* we live contradicts the message we

proclaim. The full, visible unity of God's Church is then an urgent missionary imperative, not just something to fulfil Church politics.[35]

He reiterates: "How dare we preach 'peace' to others when our own divisions cry 'hypocrite'?"; "Think of all the division in the Christian family which mocks the idea of us as a reconciled body. How dare we say with St Paul, 'be reconciled to God'… when we are so unreconciled? Isn't that a terrible contradiction of the message of the cross?"[36] In the words of Justin Welby, reconciliation is "a foretaste of the kingdom" and "makes the gospel visible". As a command of Christ, it is "not an optional extra" but "a fundamental part of the package of being saved". It is also a prominent aspect of our public witness to God's transforming power. Divisions between Christians are "desperately damaging" and a "scandal to the gospel", the archbishop declares, but a reconciled church "attracts the unbeliever" because when Christians are seen to live and work together in fellowship, despite their many disagreements, "the world sits up and takes notice".[37]

***

Questions

1. What experiences have you had of Christianity across different denominations or different theological streams?

2. Some say that "doctrine divides" while experience of God unites. Is this a helpful approach to ecumenism and Christian disagreements?

3. "The result of honest conversations between divided churches may be that different positions are shown to be incompatible and contradictory, and therefore the divisions must remain." Can this still be a form of "good disagreement"?

4. What are the benefits and problems in seeking to unite Christians around either a minimalist confession of faith (such as the World Council of Churches) or something fuller (such as the Evangelical Alliance)?

5. How would overcoming our disagreements or disagreeing better across our denominational divides help the mission of the church?

7

Good Disagreement between Religions

Toby Howarth

Disagreement occurs not only within the church, but between Christians and people of other faiths, and these can sometimes become destructive and violent. Drawing on his wide experience of interfaith relations and dialogue, Bishop Toby Howarth offers a number of lessons in this area. Illustrating his approach with concrete examples, he shows why and how Christians should seek good disagreement with followers of other religions, and how this benefits wider society. He also examines the place of evangelism and conversion from one religion to another.

It's got to be real and it's got to be good

There is much that believers from different religions rejoice to hold in common. There is also much on which we fundamentally disagree. Most of the time, communities with different beliefs get on well in societies around the world, and it doesn't make the news. When, however, religion becomes a driver or a contributor to conflict, the result can be horrific. Whether because of the violence of a suicide bomber, the genocide against a religious minority, the provocation of a Qur'an-burner or hate-preacher, or the alienation (or worse) of a convert who has left her community of faith, many people question whether good disagreement between religions is even possible, and whether bad disagreement will take us all to the kind of hell we have witnessed in Srebrenica and Syria.

The threats to good disagreement between religions are that disagreement is denied, or avoided, or handled badly. Some believe that religious disagreement is essentially illusory. If, they say, we could only see deeply enough and clearly enough the essentials of our superficially differing faiths, we would understand that really we all agree. Others try to avoid uncomfortable topics and don't want to criticize someone else's beliefs, so they skirt around the differences and end up talking in a way which, frankly, it would be hard to label as disagreement. My assumption in this chapter is that there is real, substantial difference between religions, at both a theoretical and doctrinal level and in how we live out our beliefs in our families, our neighbourhoods, and our nations. Not only do we believe and behave differently, many of us would like to see people from other religions change so that they believe and behave as we do, converting to belong to our faith community.

Substantial difference between religious believers does not, however, in my experience, inevitably lead to conflict, any more than it does between those who have different political views. Religious difference is often deeply mixed up with cultural, historical, economic, and other factors. When, therefore, conflict erupts, and because religion is such a powerful force both at a personal and public level, the violence can be particularly nasty. There are also numerous examples, however, in which religion has been part of the solution, enabling forgiveness and reconciliation where this would otherwise be unimaginable.

All Christians living in Britain today are part of a multireligious society, even if we don't have much personal contact with anyone of a different faith on a day-to-day basis. Religious disagreement is part of our daily diet in the media, and therefore in the development of our own attitudes to people of another faith including (and especially) those whom we have never met. In this context, we are called to follow Jesus, whom we call "Lord" and who taught us, quoting his own Jewish Scripture, to love our neighbours. When Jesus was asked a question about a fundamental principle of Jewish belief and practice – "What must I do to inherit eternal life?" – he answered with a positive reference to someone of another faith, a Samaritan (Luke 10:25–37). Yet Jesus was clear about the truth of his own religion, and quite capable of disagreeing with someone from another religion. As he said to another Samaritan, "You worship what you do not know; we worship what we know, for salvation is from the Jews" (John 4:22; NIV).

This chapter will reflect on examples of good religious disagreement, drawn mostly from my own personal experience, using insights from writers and other practitioners to draw out lessons for the church. It asks three questions: Why should Christians bother to seek good disagreement with followers of other religions? How does this good disagreement work itself out in wider society? What is the place of evangelism, seeking to persuade others to leave their religions and join us as followers of Jesus?

Tears and embrace: seeking good disagreement

Soon after I arrived in Bradford in 2014 as a newly consecrated bishop, I was asked to participate in the filming of an episode of BBC's *Songs of Praise*. The focus was a visit to Bradford by Mike Haines, the brother of an aid worker murdered a few months earlier by so-called "Islamic State" fighters in Iraq. Mike Haines had seen the reaction by some in the UK to the brutal murder in Woolwich, London, of a British soldier named Lee Rigby by two young men who shouted "*Allahu Akbar*" as they killed him. In the aftermath of that appalling crime, Muslim individuals, businesses, and mosques had been attacked, and Mike was determined that the legacy of his brother David's death would be different: Mike would work as hard as he could to bring Muslims, Christians, and others together in reconciliation.

After praying together in Bradford Cathedral, Mike and I went over to a mosque where the midday prayers were just finishing. While

Mike was interviewed outside, I entered the prayer room dressed in my purple shirt and bishop's cross, and spoke with one of the older men who had been worshipping. He knew that our visit was connected with the murders in Iraq and was visibly upset. Speaking in Urdu, with a younger friend interpreting for him, this man told me forcefully that those who had killed David Haines were not Muslims. In fact, he went on to claim, they were agents of Mossad or the CIA and had carried out this barbarous beheading in order to bring shame on Islam, a religion of peace. As I listened, Mike Haines walked in, was moved by the sight of the Muslim worshippers, and began to weep. Immediately the atmosphere changed. After Mike had been asked to speak, the same man embraced him with his own tears and the words, "When your brother was murdered, it was as if my whole community was beheaded."

That was an example of the complexity, seeming intransigence, and also beautiful surprise that so often marks encounters across religious divides. I was aware particularly that in my initial encounter it felt as though much more than two individuals were colliding. This Muslim elder and myself may have shared an undisputed "fact" – in this case, the video of a gruesome beheading in Iraq. The frameworks, however, within which we both understood this "fact" were quite different, coming as we did from different communities with different histories. At that point I felt as though two icebergs were crunching up against each other deep beneath the surface and preventing the two of us as individuals from coming even close to a shared understanding.

As Professor Adam Seligman, the inspiration behind the CEDAR network, puts it, "Knowledge is collective, not individual. What we know, we know collectively, as part of a group."[1] I became friends with Adam, a committed Orthodox Jew, over a period of two years in Birmingham when I worked there as a parish priest and bishop's adviser for inter-faith relations. We were part of a team bringing together with Birmingham University, over two consecutive summers, extraordinarily diverse groups of people from different religions, nations, and cultures. These groups spent a little over two weeks bumping up against each other during an intensive programme of visits, lectures, and discussion. Adam was almost attacked in his yarmulka, or Jewish skull cap, as we – Sikhs, Buddhists, Christians, and others – visited a centre for Palestinian activists in a strongly Pakistani Muslim neighbourhood shortly after the 2008–09 Gaza war. On another occasion, I wore my Anglican clerical collar as we all, including strongly conservative adherents of different religions, shared a service with the Metropolitan Community Church and heard congregation members tell of their experiences as lesbian, gay, and transgender Christians who had felt unable to worship in the fellowships in which they had grown up.

We then spent time reflecting on these experiences and learning how different the world looks from within our various "communities of belonging". We discovered that we cannot live without these communities, boundaried often by what I may eat, or wear, or say. It is within my "community of belonging" that I share a common language, history, and jokes, and it is here that I develop my individual sense of identity and worth. The crucial question is the extent to which I am prepared to extend credit or trust to someone from a different "community of belonging". Somehow, Mike Haines and the Muslim who embraced him were able to do this, creating a shared world of reference within which they could communicate with and understand one another. They did this by being prepared to communicate in a shared language of emotions and vulnerability.

Mike Haines did instinctively what many of us have had to learn and practise. The American psychologist Marshall Rosenberg has developed over many years an approach to disagreement which begins with listening for the feelings and needs behind the words of another person as a way of creating a place of shared understanding. He calls this approach Nonviolent Communication (NVC).[2] This can be difficult for people who are not used to expressing vulnerability, or who feel the need to defend their religion exclusively with a language of doctrines and ideas. NVC takes as its starting point the feelings expressed by the person with whom we disagree. Especially we are encouraged to explore what needs lie behind the feelings and how those needs are not being met.

If I ask a Jewish friend to come to church with me or to read a Gospel, I may hear in his response feelings of anxiety and discomfort. If I listen further, I may hear a need expressed around the safeguarding of his identity and his community's identity which is under threat from anti-Semitism and from assimilation into a wider, non-religious culture. I may, of course, hear something very different. It all depends on the person and their story, but it is worth listening!

Rosenberg encourages people using NVC to listen not only to others but also to their own feelings and needs. Once we understand these, we can move to the point at which requests can be made from both sides. NVC stresses the importance of making our requests clear and specific. It is much easier to negotiate specific requests that do not imply generalized judgments. NVC is a particularly good tool in helping people to practise and become adept in the kind of conversations we need in building relationships of good disagreement.

Key to both CEDAR's and NVC's approaches to good disagreement is the willingness to share the human stories behind our religious differences. When the worshipper in the mosque encountered me, he saw a "flat" picture of a man with a purple clerical shirt and a cross around his neck. That "flat" picture may have been behind his response of flat denial. Mike brought with him his more rounded story of vulnerability, expressed in his tears, and so opened up the possibility of a more "three-dimensional", nuanced response.

Story is always present in religious disagreement. Sometimes we pretend that it isn't: we talk about our disagreement as if it was a pure, rational discussion of the mind. In my experience, male religious leaders are particularly prone to addressing difference in this way. We look at texts; we discuss doctrines. While this is an important, even essential, aspect of inter-religious dialogue, it often needs to be complemented by the sharing of our human stories.

The struggle to "fill out" our perceptions of other people in the face of strong disagreement has been a particular feature for me of meetings of the Hindu Christian Forum. This Forum has developed innovative and creative ways of bringing people together across our two religious communities at a local level (such as an inter-religious event based around the stories of women boxers). At a national level, however, its leaders have struggled with the burden of representing and including people who perceive the other community in sometimes very negative ways as a result of the history of difficult relationships in India.

Some Hindus see Christians as the inheritors or representatives of churches which have been involved in forced conversions and a colonial attempt to define Hinduism negatively. Even the concept of "Hinduism" is perceived as a creation of Western scholars and missionaries.[3] Western church leaders on the other hand, keen to express solidarity with their sister churches in India, want to bring the often life and death issues for those churches to the table, especially concerning caste discrimination and religious persecution. Accusations and counter-accusations with hyped-up language linked to grainy videos fly around cyberspace. There may be some exaggeration, but there is also a dark reality behind the rhetoric. Even a cursory visit to some of those web pages reveals how easy it is to live in our own, Internet-fed worlds, reinforcing our own victimhoods without meeting as people and sharing our individual stories.

In our Forum meetings, we have tried to "fill out" our understandings of each other by committing to hearing some of the personal family histories and faith stories which lie behind the positions we take. This process has needed strong leadership. Soon after Justin Welby became Archbishop of Canterbury and stated that one of his priorities in office would be to strengthen the evangelism and witness of the church, he agreed to meet with the Hindu

Christian Forum, a number of whom were not best pleased at this priority. I remember him sitting at the table in his shirt sleeves with the empty page of a large notebook before him, and simply asking those present to share while he listened and took notes. He then asked his staff, including his Director of Evangelism and Witness, to go on listening and to continue the discussions with the Forum. Similarly, when disagreement threatened to break down the Forum's work entirely, one of the Hindu members simply asked all of us around the table to come to his home and to share a meal with him and his family.

Even our doctrines have their own stories. Often the doctrine of the Trinity is presented by Christians to others as a "flat" statement of belief, maybe explained a little in terms of ice, water, and steam or some other theoretical device. While this can be helpful, it does not do justice to the way in which that doctrine developed within the church. The Trinity as a doctrine became understood over time and sometimes painfully by Jesus' disciples, strict monotheists who encountered at close hand a man they came to see as the human face of God. Later, these people had a powerful experience at Pentecost, which they understood with reference to their own, Jewish Scriptures, as being an experience of God's Spirit. Christians didn't sit down one day around a kettle and some ice-cubes and decide it would be nice to believe in the Trinity! Rather we believe that understanding was given to us, revealed as the Scriptures bear witness. But the church's mature articulation of that revelation came about through years of experience, reflection, and prayer. It is vital, therefore, that Christians learn to give an account of their faith in relation both to that early story of the disciples and to their own personal stories and experiences.

Similarly, it has helped me in trying to understand the Islamic doctrine of *tawhid*, or the sheer "unicity" of God, as I have read and listened to Muslims explaining their narrative of how Islam was revealed into a context of tribal polytheism. Against that backdrop, the attempt to "ascribe a partner to God" is considered by Muslims generally to be the greatest and the unforgivable sin. If the Christian doctrine of the Trinity is heard as a kind of polytheism in that mould, it may provoke deep hostility. A religious education teacher told me recently of his experience trying to explain the Christian doctrine of the Trinity as part of the syllabus to a class of secondary-school-age Muslims. Two of the otherwise well-behaved boys in the class were so incensed with the diagram he had shown of the Trinity that they tried to tear it down.

Each year, a series of academic seminars called "Building Bridges" have brought together Christian and Muslim scholars to engage in the painstaking and at the same time exciting work of drilling down into our doctrinal disagreements, untangling history and nuances through the detailed study of texts. The seminars are run by Georgetown University in Washington, DC, previously in partnership with Lambeth Palace in London, and have addressed a wide range of topics. These include Muslim and Christian understandings of prophecy, science and religion, justice and human rights, as well as death and the afterlife. These textual studies are academically rigorous while taking place in the context of shared meals and shared friendships. The former Archbishop of Canterbury Rowan Williams, who personally convened many of the seminars, ended one of his first with the memorable words, "We have disagreed well…"

Foundational to the different approaches that I have referred to here is a commitment to the often slow and painstaking work of developing relationships, especially by listening to the other person's story and sharing one's own. On the one hand, this can seem a frustrating acknowledgment that there is no quick fix to overcoming religious difference. On the other, even small bridges built can carry surprisingly heavy loads. The gesture that Mike Haines made in entering the mosque and weeping with the Muslim worshippers not only brought him and them to a new level of communication and understanding, it also enabled me and others to travel along that road ourselves.

"Seek the peace of the city": good religious disagreement in our wider society

Christians have a clear calling to reach out beyond their comfort zones, beyond their own "communities of belonging", to engage positively with people of different faiths with whom they disagree. But the Christian calling to promote "good disagreement" does not stop there. The prophet Jeremiah wrote to the small Jewish community exiled in Babylon challenging them to pray and work for the peace of the places within which they found themselves (Jeremiah 29). Jesus called his followers to be "salt and light" (Matthew 5:13–16), promoting good, healthy relationships in their neighbourhoods. Obedience to that biblical teaching involves encouraging and enabling good disagreement within our own multireligious society even beyond our own circle of relationships.

The Church of England has a particular calling in this regard, with bishops in the House of Lords and an engagement with wider society that is enshrined in law. Part of the responsibility of being an established church is a strong commitment to positive interfaith relationships across our society and a willingness to commit resources to this work at all levels. In Britain there is a vast network of good relationships, but also an increasing amount of fear. Some religious leaders propagate doctrines and ideologies specifically designed to keep their followers separate. But in my experience, both within and outside the Church of England, Christians are well placed to offer spaces in which others can meet and build relationships with those who believe differently and with whom they may profoundly disagree.

In 2014 a document known as "Trojan Horse" achieved notoriety in Birmingham, alleging a plot on the part of a group of Muslim activists to "take over" the governance of a number of state schools in the city with high proportions of Muslim pupils. It was believed that these schools were then encouraged to promote an ethos based on a particular, conservative vision of Islam that, among other things, encouraged separation from wider British society, made it harder for boys and girls to mix together, and discouraged the study of music and drama.

The reaction to "Trojan Horse" became hugely political even at a national level, with the media camped outside particular schools and yet further negative profiling of Muslim communities in the city and more widely. But the issues raised by the media interest and the various reports commissioned to find out what had really taken place were important ones for our wider society. The Bishop of Birmingham's response was to convene a series of "Birmingham Conversations". A carefully chosen group of twenty-four people from a range of religious, ethnic, and social backgrounds, balanced across age and gender, were invited to commit to meeting every month over six months to address the question "What does lived faith look like in a twenty-first-century city?" The aim of these conversations was precisely to learn together to "disagree well". There was no attempt to "solve" problems by leading everyone to believe the same thing or to act in the same way. Instead, a trained facilitator from Birmingham University worked with the participants to help them hear and understand the "back stories" that had led them to hold widely differing views in a common, shared city space.

Birmingham has also been one of several areas of the country to roll out a programme called Near Neighbours. This is a partnership between the government and the Church of England's Church Urban Fund, working at multiple levels to help bring neighbours from different religious and cultural backgrounds together for the common good. Small grants are offered to local groups and projects, but these groups have to show that they represent more than one "community of belonging" and that the project proposal has been developed jointly. Although the grants are administered (with considerable speed) by the Church Urban Fund, they may fund a project with no Christian involvement, for example between Jewish and Muslim women. Near Neighbours also funds other initiatives, such as Catalyst, a programme that brings young leaders from different faiths together, and The Feast, which works creatively with secondary-school-age children, particularly Christians and Muslims.

The work of Near Neighbours is built on a commitment to work with difference and disagreement to a common end. Like the "Birmingham Conversations", it does not aim for participants to "leave their hats at the door", in the phrase popularized by Rowan Williams. We do not have to remove our yarmulkas or turbans in order to enter and participate in the "public square" of our common civic life. There may be a difficult discussion about how much of the face is covered by a particular piece of headgear in a particular context such as a primary school classroom, but our religious identity and behaviour does not have to be replaced by a secular way of operating before we are allowed to contribute to the common life of our nation.

I have seen different models, theories, and approaches worked out and reflected upon over the years in which I have been involved in inter-religious relations. The Citizens Organising Movement, for example, builds coalitions of different groups, led often by strong inter-religious partnerships, empowering people, especially those marginalized by political processes, to take back the power that should be theirs as citizens. Schools Linking, another example, uses Intergroup Contact Theory as a basis for its powerful work enabling children and teachers from primary schools in very different contexts to get to know each other. Contact Theory argues that deep differences between communities will lead to conflict unless certain conditions are put in place. These conditions include the different parties having equal status, common goals, the support of external authorities, and the opportunity to engage personally with each other. I have found it moving to see young children from inner-city Bradford meet up at an art gallery with others from sharply contrasting ethnic, religious, and social backgrounds in order to work in creative and fun ways on deep issues of identity and shared values. The skills that these children are learning include a capacity to disagree well with each other in a way that gives hope for a city and region still very divided.

The Contact Theory condition of supportive external authorities raises an important issue when we consider good disagreement between religions. At a certain point, no matter how well we understand one another and each other's stories, law-makers and the judiciary will need to make judgment calls about whether a particular practice can be tolerated or not. Rowan Williams argues for a society made up of "a community of communities" with the state acting as a structure which can organize and mediate between them. The state's task is to encourage a rich fabric of civil society in which all can flourish as much as possible. There will be times, however, when the state may have to intervene if one of these communities seeks to impose its will on others in a way that is destructive to another community or to that shared environment.[4]

An extremely complex and difficult issue concerns the religious slaughter of animals for food. Many Jews and Muslims in particular may, according to their religious laws, only eat animals that have been slaughtered without having been pre-stunned, and they have been able to campaign together on this issue. The stakes are high: how as a society do we balance concerns, including religious concerns, for the welfare of animals with the internationally acknowledged right for people and communities to follow their religious beliefs and practices? The issue becomes even more acute, again particularly for Jews and Muslims, when some argue that the circumcision of male babies represents an infringement of the rights of those children and should be banned by law. This would result in Muslims, Jews, and others who are obligated under their religious laws to practise circumcision feeling ostracized.

Good religious disagreement, then, is important for religious people and communities as we thrash out among ourselves the boundaries we are willing to tolerate for our differences. It is important also for our wider society as we debate the legal limits on each other's behaviour. But even when we decide as a society to move in a particular direction, we have to remain conscious of those who are left behind. Drawing on an extraordinary mix of Aristotle and the American novelist Ralph Ellison, classics professor Danielle Allen argues for "antagonistic cooperation" between communities with deeply conflicting interests.[5] One of the problems she addresses is what happens when a society, on the basis of majority rule, imposes its will on a minority community. Unless the majority takes seriously the sacrifice made by this minority in remaining within the wider society, our common civic "home" can feel to the minority like a place of oppression. We need limits on behaviour, such as acts of violence or hate speech that endangers others. Nevertheless, it is arguably a failure to attend to the "sacrifice", in this sense, of young Muslims who profoundly disagree with aspects of British foreign and domestic policy yet remain part of our communities, that has contributed to the alienation that many feel, and the appalling actions of a very few.

"Go and make disciples": persuasion and conversion

Christians have a clear calling from Scripture to work for peace in their society and to learn to disagree well with those who hold views that conflict with their own. This, however, is not our only calling. Jesus says in the Gospels, "Blessed are the peacemakers" (Matthew 5:9). He also says, "Go and make disciples of all nations, baptising them in the name of the Father and of the Son and of the Holy Spirit" (Matthew 28:19; NIV). Does good disagreement between religions allow room for trying to persuade somebody of a different faith to embrace mine?

For some, these two callings are simply incompatible with one another. Many Hindus would understand any attempt to convert them to Christianity or Islam as something akin to asking a person to change their mother. Our religious affiliation is often such a deep part of our identity that any desire to persuade someone to change it is assumed to be deeply hurtful. But in other areas of life we take a very different view. I may have been a committed, paid-up member of a political party all my life, but nobody would bat an eyelid in the run-up to an election if somebody knocked on my door and attempted to persuade me to vote differently this time around. Similarly, in our educational system much of our learning is predicated on being able to persuade others to change their minds, often in areas which matter a great deal.

Many Muslims, Buddhists, atheists, and even some who are part of the wider Hindu community such as the International Society for Krishna Consciousness, feel no embarrassment in asking people to leave their old beliefs and embrace something new. Why then are so many Christians embarrassed about trying to persuade others to convert to Christianity? Article 18 of the Universal Declaration of Human Rights (adopted by the United Nations in 1948) enshrines the freedom of thought, conscience, and religion, including the right to change one's religion. Without the freedom to change religion, the freedom to believe would be meaningless.

Some Christians worry that evangelism in a multi-faith context is incompatible with "good disagreement" and leads inevitably to conflict. But not all conflict is destructive. Although many would like to see the floor of the House of Commons a less adversarial place, we generally understand the conflict of ideas that takes place at the heart of our democracy as something healthy. As long as evangelism and conversion are governed by strong ethical principles, we should not be afraid of them. The basic biblical injunction to love our neighbour as ourselves goes a long way in this regard. If we want to negotiate difference, we need to learn not to avoid it but rather to persuade others well. This involves becoming a trustworthy person, formulating an argument that speaks to people where they are and being as persuasive as possible. But it also involves being clear that the choice of action belongs to the listener.

A particularly helpful, and indeed groundbreaking, document from the Christian Muslim Forum is entitled "Ethical Guidelines for Christian and Muslim Witness in Britain" (2009). It begins with a short preamble acknowledging that while Christians and Muslims are committed to working together for the common good, many from both faiths are also active in inviting others to change their religion.

The document aims to provide not a theology but rather guidance for good practice. It commits those who have signed up to it from both religions, among other things, to avoid any sharing of the faith which is coercive, particularly in regard to children, young people, and vulnerable adults. It shuns any invitation to convert that is linked to financial or material inducements. Ridiculing or demeaning another person's faith is ruled out, as is forcing anyone who wishes to leave the community of faith to remain.

In many ways, sharing our faith with someone from another religious tradition will look the same as sharing with someone from a nominal Christian background or of no faith at all. Hopefully there will be real dialogue: a deep listening as well as sharing. The context will most often be a friendship in which there is a commitment to our friend as a person with a story and a "community of belonging". There will be a concern to listen for how the Christian message is "good news" for our friend, a deep respect for her freedom to choose, and an acknowledgment that conversion across religious boundaries may be costly.

Christian witness is not just limited to personal conversations and friendships. I was once asked to attend and speak at a gathering of about 1,000 Muslims who had come to hear an internationally well-known spiritual leader and preacher. The gathering was partly a celebration of the life of the Prophet Muhammad, and there were a number of "warm-up" speakers. There is sometimes an expectation at these occasions that non-Muslim visitors will speak positively about Muhammad, in a vague sense tacitly endorsing the rest of the proceedings. There had, that day, been a terrible attack reported in the international news by terrorists acting in the name of Islam who had specifically targeted Christians, and none of the speakers previous to myself had mentioned this attack.

I felt therefore that I needed to mention the atrocity, for not to do so would have been dishonest to my presence there as a Christian leader. I spoke briefly from the passage in Mark's Gospel in which Jesus healed a man on the sabbath but his opponents used the healing as an excuse to accuse him. Jesus' response, we are told, was powerful: "He looked around at them with anger" (Mark 3:5). I said that I thought Jesus was angry because those religious leaders were focusing on a divisive distraction in the face of clear human need. I went on to say that for me as a Christian, Jesus is the human face of God and therefore when Jesus is angry I understand that God is angry. And because of the way Jesus acted in this Gospel story, I believe that God is angry at what happened in that terrorist incident. Of course, we are appalled at any violent taking of life. But there is particular anger when in the context of poverty and oppression, people focus on dividing communities along religious lines rather than fighting the poverty and oppression itself.

The speaker who followed me spent considerable time indirectly criticizing what I had said on the grounds that I had promoted the unforgivable sin (in Islamic terms) of "associating a partner with God", presumably by saying that Jesus was the human face of God. In any case, I had to examine my own conscience as to whether I had been out of place in speaking as I did, a guest at a particularly holy occasion. It is still a question for me. What I was trying to do in that gathering, however flawed the outcome, was to be faithful to my calling as a Christian leader, the basis on which I had been invited. I had set out not to demean the faith of my hosts, but rather to hold out a distinctive Christian view of Jesus in order that my listeners might understand not only what Jesus means to us in the church, but how that understanding speaks into our shared world.

Jesus and a Samaritan woman together model good disagreement between religions in their conversation at a well told in John's Gospel (chapter 4). There is real vulnerability on both of their parts: hers in taking on a rabbi in theological debate, and his in asking for a drink from a person and a bucket that would have made him unclean in the eyes of many from his own religious community. There is a willingness to share personally and a shunning of superficial religious competitiveness ("my temple is better than your temple") in favour of a desire to engage deeply with what God requires.

There is also persuasion in this story and a willingness to change. The woman and her village community are persuaded that this Jew is indeed Messiah and the "Saviour of the world". Her joy and her village's openness in turn persuade Jesus to remain there overnight, breaking with his own traditions to receive their religiously tainted hospitality. The very early Christian community, in telling and retelling this story, found joy themselves as their own ethnic boundaries were painfully broken in welcoming Gentiles into the community of faith. They found that God is present, in Christ, as the walls come down.

One reason that religious disagreement is often so painful is precisely that religious believers do have so much in common. Our very closeness makes our differences that much sharper. This is the experience of the patriarch Jacob and his brother Esau in the book of Genesis. In that story Jacob, having cheated his brother out of his birthright, runs away to stay with an uncle. But he can't remain in exile forever and, at a certain point, he is called by God to return to the land of promise, with Esau standing in the way. Jacob, we are told, is "greatly afraid and distressed" (Genesis 32:7). On the night before they meet, he is confronted by a mysterious divine combatant with whom he wrestles until dawn. Then, the following day, he is confronted with his estranged brother, Esau, who embraces him with tears. After the first encounter, Jacob says, "I have seen the face of God and lived" (Genesis 32:30). At the second, he says to his brother, "To see you is to see the face of God" (Genesis 33:10). The encounters leave Jacob with a wound, a limp. Neither of them, as the story goes on, feels conclusive. Reconciliation is not complete. But the narrative has made clear, in the words of Professor Walter Brueggemann, that "On the way to *his brother...* Jacob must deal with *his God*".[6] One could put it the other way around: on the way to his God, Jacob must deal with his brother.

The territory in which we explore good disagreement can be bruising and inconclusive; it may bring fear and weeping, but hopefully an embrace. We venture there as Christians not just because it is a good thing to do, or even a necessary thing given the state of our world. We venture into this territory because we are called by God to meet God there, because God is waiting for us there. To quote Jacob again, "This is none other than the house of God; this is the gate of heaven" (Genesis 28:17; NIV).

***

Questions

1. Have you had experiences – good or bad – of disagreeing with those of other religions?

2. Why does religious difference and disagreement often lead to conflict? How can we prevent this happening?

3. From your own experience and the stories given in this chapter, how can Christians work with those of other faiths to benefit wider society?

4. What role should the state have in mediating between religions?

5. Do you agree that "good disagreement" can and should include a place for conversion between religions? What are the implications for the church's mission?

8

From Castles to Conversations: Reflections on How to Disagree Well

Lis Goddard and Clare Hendry

Lis Goddard and Clare Hendry are both ordained Anglican clergy: Lis is a priest/presbyter with oversight of a parish, Clare a deacon. They are co-authors of *The Gender Agenda* (IVP, 2010) in which they dialogue with each other about their differences over what the Bible teaches about women's leadership within the church. Here they reflect on their experience of working together to explore their disagreement and highlight some of the wider lessons and questions about "good disagreement" arising out of their conversations.

Beginning to talk

Lis: In the summer of 2004 our family took a holiday on the coast of Donegal. I broke our cardinal rule not to take any work and read two pre-publication manuscripts from a Christian publisher addressing the question of the limits on women's roles within the church. They were extremely well written and very good scholarship but as I read I became increasingly downhearted. The serious problem was that both masterly tomes read as though they were written from a very well-defended castle, built across the valley from another very well-defended castle. Each had all its ammunition set out along its battlements and the books were the display of the ammunition – lobbing rocks over the walls at each other, firing arrows. But neither castle's inhabitants had considered the possibility that talking to the other was an option – that exploring the enemy's territory might be helpful, seeing whether there were in fact some points of similarity and solidarity. The impression was that this was out of the question – the other viewpoint was so beyond the pale that to talk, to engage directly with those who held it, was unthinkable. For me this was heartbreakingly sad and seemed to do the church no favours.

It seemed to exemplify much of what was going on across the church – so much shouting from highly fortified castles, lobbing rocks across the chasm, but very little serious engagement or willingness to treat the other as someone to listen to, sit with and really try to understand. I longed for this to change. If we were to work through this issue and continue to serve God together, preaching the gospel, we had to learn how to keep talking to each other, why the other thought as they did, and most importantly why they read Scripture as they did.

This was particularly important for me. I had grown up in a solidly biblical conservative evangelical clergy family, where I had been constantly encouraged, like my three brothers, to fulfil my potential. But I always knew that one thing I could never do was be ordained. When I got to university I realized that people thought differently and I had to start to engage with those different views. There could be no ghettoizing; we had to do this together. We studied Scripture together, men and women, those who were conservative on this issue and those who were not. We read books – everything we could lay our hands on. We wrote each other papers and, most importantly, we prayed with and for each other and learned to trust each other, deeply.

Through that process I learned some very important lessons which have stayed with me throughout my life. Perhaps the most important is that you should always talk and engage with others. Shouting across chasms is never healthy or helpful. I don't always get this right, but it has become my gold standard. I also discovered something which has changed the whole course of my life: to my surprise, I discovered that I was convinced that Scripture, rather than forbidding women to lead congregations and teach the Bible, in fact encouraged and released women into these callings. I also learned that when trying to engage people with a difficult subject you are much better to learn to talk their language, to speak into their context and their fears, to make it real and personal.

So, when IVP asked whether I would be willing to write a book with someone who disagreed with me on the whole question of women's leadership I couldn't say no. I wanted to show that it was possible to meet in the valley between the castles; that it was possible to work through the disagreement and build a friendship. Looking for someone who might be willing to go on this journey with me I asked Clare Hendry who served with me on the committee of AWESOME, a group to support, equip, and speak for evangelical ordained women particularly within the Church of England.

Clare: My path into ministry was somewhat different. I grew up in a non-Christian home and came to faith through the Christian Union at school. I was all set on a path into teaching when I ended up studying for a Masters in a seminary in the United States. I became convinced that God was calling me to work in the area of pastoral counselling in the Anglican Church. The only way that seemed possible was to go forward for ordination but that door initially closed and in 1986 I started lecturing in an Anglican theological college. This was before women were able to be priested but the discussions were in full flow. I soon became aware of what different groups within the church believed, especially with regards to headship of the local church.

I grew frustrated at times with hearing discussions but then not seeing the same people or churches actually following through and encouraging women to fulfil whatever role they believed the Bible taught. Like Lis, I also believed that the Bible encouraged women to teach and be in leadership. Where we differed was exactly what that looked like and who could be the main leader in a local church.

I believe, from careful study of the Scriptures, that a man should lead the local church and also that the husband should be head of his household. The way that has worked out in ministry for me is that I have served on leadership teams in churches with a male vicar. I think that in the Bible there are cases where women have taught (e.g. Acts 18:24–26) and been involved in leadership but always with a man in ultimate authority. I have occasionally preached but clearly under the authority of the male vicar. What I have sought to do is to ensure that I do not undermine what I believe is the biblical pattern of male headship, though some taking my (complementarian) position on headship would apply it differently.

As I listened to various groups, both egalitarian and complementarian,[1] three things struck me about the way people across the divides held their position: there was a failure to engage with the biblical texts, a failure to engage with the people holding the opposing view, and a lack of grace and love shown to those who did not agree with their position. When Lis asked if I would write with her it was therefore exciting and challenging. I felt rather out of my comfort zone as I saw myself more as a pastoral theologian than a biblical scholar and knew I was potentially opening myself up to a lot of flak from some who would strongly disagree with me. But here was a project that gave me the opportunity to contribute something positive to the debate, to engage and interact with someone I disagreed with as we explored biblical passages, modelling grace and humility as we listened to each other.

Does how we disagree matter?

Lis: One passage which has become increasingly important to me is "I have given them the glory that you gave me, that they may be one as we are one – I in them and you in me – so that they may be brought to complete unity. Then the world will know that you sent me and have loved them even as you have loved me" (John 17:22–23; NIV). It is not enough to have right doctrine or to preach the gospel. We must also learn to pray Christ's prayer for his church in John 17 and live it out. This is vital not just for our own health, but also for the world's fundamental health and well-being. The massive challenge is how we hold the profound truth of God's world-changing, transforming and transfiguring, unifying love in tension with the gospel of repentance and foundational doctrines. I have seen so many instances of people disagreeing with little grace or understanding of the unity mandate.

As we dialogued, Clare and I were aware of how much we could be giving away if we weren't careful. I believe we are called to work with God to overcome even the most profound divisions but at times I found myself asking whether I was giving away too much. For example, we speak about the "gospel" being the main thing, but what do we mean by that? Clearly we mean forgiveness, freedom, and redemption in Christ and through his death. Clare and I totally agreed on that. I think where we disagreed and I found myself wondering about its significance was that I would also say the gospel includes the restoration of creation order and for me that has profound implications for male–female relations and for the church. I cannot speak about salvation without wanting to speak about that too. As we wrote the book, I think we both knew there was this difference between us, but, out of love, we chose to speak of the "gospel" in terms we both understood. I did it because it is not wrong, just not as complex as the reality, and because God's unifying love calls us to act in grace, as he does.

Clare: We had both experienced and witnessed bad disagreement and so were committed to modelling how to disagree in a gracious and loving manner. So often Christians have done the gospel a disservice in how they have publicly disagreed: showing little grace, humility, and love and being critical and condemning those who don't agree. The world sees how some Christians behave in unpleasant public disagreements, often over what it sees as trivial or irrelevant things, and, not surprisingly, wants little to do with Christianity. Tragically, as people reject the Christianity they see, they also reject Christ. Yet the gospel at its very heart models a very different way of relating when you disagree. Throughout the New Testament we are encouraged where possible to live at peace with each other (Hebrews 12:14). As God's people we should live in a way that is honouring to God and, as those raised with Christ, live distinctive lives being compassionate, humble, gentle, bearing with each other, relating in a way that builds up the church (Colossians 3:12–14).

Disagreement and Scripture

Lis: We are both women called to ministry and Christian leadership, and yet we disagree profoundly over what that looks like. We found that as we wrestled with these and other issues, we were both clear that our baseline had to be Scripture. As pastoral theologians we are well versed in theological reflection and the reflective cycle in which one asks "How can I relate life to theology and theology to life?" We have too often seen people stuck in their reflective cycle on, in the words of a friend, "insipid self-reflection" which they called theology. True, solid, good theological reflection never stops with experience, or with "me", but is always challenged by God, by Scripture. It lays itself open to be changed, whatever the cost of that might be. For us, good disagreement was based on mutual trust that the other person was as open to the challenge of God in Scripture as we were.

Clare: I knew we were both starting from the same position, under Scripture's authority. If we spoke only from our experience, and allowed that to be our authority for holding the positions we did, it would be unworkable. It closes down conversation, as we would either hold back from saying things because we didn't want to hurt each other or end up undermining each other. We needed a reference point from which we could evaluate what we both thought and believed, and that had to be God's word. Because we were both allowing our experience to come under its authority it was possible to be honest and vulnerable, to trust each other and properly engage and debate with each other.

A particularly tricky challenge was not allowing our disagreement to get "personal", while acknowledging that actually it is intensely personal. This was what we felt God was calling us to as women in ministry, so it was not theoretical. It wasn't even that one could say, "Well, I feel God has called me to be a vicar", and the other, "Great, well that's good for you, but I feel called more to a supportive assistant type role." There was the sense of personal calling, but our disagreement was also tied up with what we thought the Bible taught. We could talk back and forth about these deeply personal issues precisely because we had agreed to respect each other's opinions and we knew we were both trying to base our understanding on the Bible, albeit that we disagreed at times over exactly what the Bible teaches.

We were able to dialogue because of our commitment to trusting and respecting one another. In other situations people disagreeing with my position have written me off and shown no willingness to hear what I am saying. Often there is not a desire on their part really to seek what the Bible is teaching. In those situations there is no sense of unity in the gospel, and partnership in proclaiming the gospel seems impossible. The walls just seem to be built up further, and from the world's view it just confirms their belief that Christianity has nothing to offer.

Learning trust, vulnerability, and respect

Lis: Writing a book could be seen as a task, rather cerebral and not needing real, personal investment. But the reality was and remains that we were dealing with something precious and vulnerable. It is not good enough to set out one's case aggressively, polemically, regardless of the hurt or damage caused. It would be so easy to batter, rather than to listen. We are often far too ready to speak, and poor at listening to another's point of view.

We wrote the book through an email correspondence, which allowed the other person time to respond carefully to points made. There was no room for talking over the other or dismissing their viewpoint. Listening makes you think, challenges and unsettles you, and ultimately throws you back on to God and his word. On several occasions Clare responded and said things I really wasn't expecting – I thought I knew what she thought, what she would say, but I was wrong, and I had to think, read, and pray hard before I replied. I also became aware that this cut very close for Clare as it did for me, affecting her marriage, her vocation, her mothering, her self-understanding. It was holy ground, and I needed to be so careful how I spoke and wrote.

Clare: Respect for each other and a willingness to listen and to try to hear what the other person is saying is the key to being able to disagree well. I would like to say it was easy but it wasn't always. I sometimes got frustrated when Lis's reply to my latest email felt unjustified. For instance when she expressed sadness because she felt overwhelmed that I had denied the women in the Old Testament their rightful achievements. I felt that did not represent what I was doing (and I am sure Lis also got frustrated by some of my emails).

Both of us were sometimes tempted to take pot shots and score points, to be less than gracious when we responded to something the other was saying with which we "violently" disagreed. We had to work at it, asking God to help us to be truly open to hearing what the other person was saying, rather than dismissing it in our head because it was not what we thought or because we wanted to win the argument and come out on top! Humility and love had to be guiding principles for our discussions, along with a commitment to hear not only each other but what God was saying.

Lis: Respect could only mean something if we trusted each other person. This meant a willingness to allow Clare into my experience, not just to throw out arguments and "killer one-liners". I had to invite her into what it is like to be me, seeking to live with this calling, and to trust her not to dismiss it but to engage with me respectfully and with a willingness to learn. This meant sharing our lives and ministries, getting to know each other well, and understanding what it means to walk the walk God has called each of us to. That could make each of us feel very vulnerable because we knew the other had questions about decisions which had shaped our lives, but we made a decision to trust in love. If you are going to journey into the uncharted waters of trying to understand the other, you need to invest in getting to know them properly.

This decision to entrust our lives to each other was helped because although it was inevitably very personal we both decided we would not take what the other said personally. We would listen carefully and seriously to the other, allowing what they said to challenge us to re-think our conclusions but not allowing what they said, when it inevitably challenged our life choices, to become a personal attack. Clare and I, for example, also disagree about how Ephesians 5:21– 33 should be read and applied within a Christian marriage. I could easily have taken her clear and honest comments on how she thinks God has designed Christian marriages to be structured as a personal criticism, even though they weren't meant that way. I made a very deliberate decision not to do this and although it was not always easy to live this out it was vital that we did.

We also each tried not to speak or write personally and when we did we were quick to apologize. At one point I described one of Clare's ideas as "bizarre". She rightly pulled me up on it, and in my next email I apologized and acknowledged that was unacceptable. It was an idea which made – and still makes – no sense to me, but we were discussing a point and trying to be as open as possible to the other's point of view, enabling them to speak freely, doing them the honour of taking them seriously and not dismissing them.

Clare: As we committed to taking the other seriously it had challenging, even scary implications. We had to be willing for God's word to change us. So in practice what might that have meant?

Recognizing we were wrong would have had implications for both of us. It could have changed the view we held on women's ministry and therefore our own ministry. I could have found I was convicted that the weight of the biblical passages was on the side of saying that women could lead a local church. In many ways for me changing my position would not have closed doors in the way that it might have for Lis. However, I think that some people in groups that I am part of might have felt that I was going down the wrong path and lost confidence in me, so they might have stopped inviting me to give talks or referring anyone to me for counselling.

For Lis it would have dramatically changed what she is currently involved in. She would not be vicar at St James the Less, and it would have had implications for chairing AWESOME and being involved with various other groups where she supports women in ministry. Engaging with people who disagree with you is not always easy and can be costly, but that must not be a reason for avoiding it.

The highs and lows of disagreeing well

Lis: This sort of conversation about disagreements is tiring on every level: emotionally, physically, and spiritually. There is something exhausting about ensuring that you are doing justice to your own arguments and reasoning and those of the person you are talking to. That means a discipline of listening well to get inside their thinking, to engage with their scriptural hermeneutic, and to understand how they relate to God in prayer, worship, and Bible study. It is exhausting to allow oneself to be challenged and to take that challenge well and seriously, particularly when the subject goes to the very heart of one's calling and self-understanding in God, and yet not allow it to be personal.

There were several points where I had to think, pray, and study very hard, to allow God to work with me, to allow myself to be in a place of uncertainty. If I am honest, the work of disagreeing well with Clare was made harder because some people didn't understand why I was doing it; why it was important to get out of the castle and stop lobbing rocks. Some challenged me hard that there were people whom you should just not talk to, that it was selling the pass, that if you disagree, you disagree and that is it. That was very hard. I completely understood where they were coming from, but I believe we always have to talk to try to understand the other, if only so that we can *disagree* well. I will always hold that we have to be godly in our disagreement, and that means listening and getting to know the other. I can anticipate situations where I may conclude that someone is profoundly wrong, but I cannot anticipate circumstances where I would regret getting to know them, spending time listening, allowing myself to be challenged to return to Scripture and to my knees.

Having said all this, it can also be exhilarating: I loved writing the book with Clare. There is something very special about walking this sort of journey with another human being, working hard at understanding someone else, at hearing them, exploring their thoughts with them, being allowed that sort of access, knowing that they have travelled that journey with you. It is such a privilege to get to know someone else so very well, to find so much that we agree on, such as when we corresponded on Mary, the mother of Jesus, and it was remarkable how much in accord we were, both finding her an amazing role model.

Clare: I would echo much of what Lis has said about the highs and lows. There were times when it was a struggle, when I read what she had written and it challenged me on what I had previously understood a passage of Scripture to mean. There were one or two passages where I thought that it could be read either way. That led to a lot of soul-searching as I wanted to make sure I was open to being changed by God's word. There were times when I felt I wasn't explaining myself particularly well. I passionately believed in my position. It hadn't been something that I had come to lightly, and

I wanted to make sure that I gave a clear account of why I had interpreted a particular passage as I did, so people did not think my position was wrong because I'd not explained it properly.

The experience was also a source of blessing and joy. It was a privilege to interact with someone on an issue which was so important for both of us but in a way that felt safe, where we trusted each other and were committed to making it work. We both came out of it understanding and appreciating each other's position better and seeing how much we did have in common through the gospel. We shared not just our positions on this issue, but also something of our lives as, at different times in the writing process, we both experienced challenging times in our ministries. Finally, it was a joy to read the reviews and see that what we had set out to achieve through the writing of the book seemed to have worked.

Transforming disagreement?

Lis: That does not mean that we don't disagree – I still think that Clare is wrong on this issue – but it does mean that I acknowledge that I could be the one in the wrong and in engaging with her I am seeking her good. It was vital to me that through our engagement and friendship I should seek her flourishing. That meant working honestly with her to engage with Scripture, as it is in Christ and our deepening knowledge of his will for our lives, and more fully aligning ourselves to that will, that we become who we were created to be. It also meant a willingness to acknowledge my vulnerability, my inadequacy. I have in my Bible a card which says "I could be wrong", as a reminder that none of us has a monopoly on the truth, that each of us can only be faithful as far as we are able, but that it is in seeking to know God better that we are transformed into the likeness of Christ.

I have always understood it to be my responsibility to do my best to enable others to be transformed more and more into the image and glory of Christ. The gospel demands that I don't get on my high horse and refuse to work with people because they don't fit my needs for affirmation as a woman in leadership. As a chaplain at Oxford University, I regularly worked with student groups I knew would never let me preach because I was a woman, but they were sharing Christ with their friends and that was much more important. I also used the opportunities it gave me to challenge them where I thought they were wrong and to engage in good conversations with them in ways that allowed each of us to explore honestly and openly what Scripture says.

I believe that I am called to listen and to engage well, not just to walk away. Good disagreement means exploring properly, getting to the roots of where the disagreement lies. It may at some point involve walking apart but this is a last resort, when all options have been exhausted. Generally it involves finding ways of blessing the other and enabling them, as far as it lies within my power, to become more like Jesus and to share the gospel faithfully. I suppose that the rub comes if these last two are not possible – if the other person is determined to push back against the challenge to Christlikeness and the transforming gospel-sharing we are exploring. There would then be all sorts of questions to ask about where the similarities in our faith began and ended.

Clare: I think that our book and way of disagreeing has helped promote more engagement between the two positions and encouraged people to listen to each other more carefully. There is less shouting across the chasm and more listening and debate in a way that helps promote unity and models grace and humility. Some have been challenged about heart issues: What is their motive for engaging in debate? How much is the way they do it affected by wanting to win the argument or by pride?

For example, I have for years been involved with the Fellowship of Word and Spirit, a group of mainly ordained Anglicans on the more conservative side of the theological spectrum who are committed to helping people apply Reformed theology in the local church. Their conferences have always been places where debate is encouraged, and there is a strong sense of fellowship and support for ministers. Not everyone in that group agrees with how I work out the principle of male headship in ministry, but they are always gracious and willing to listen. I have seen a growing commitment to listen to those who either apply the headship principle in a different way or hold a completely different position on headship.

In the long term I hope that our model encourages Christians to listen to each other more graciously and present a better witness to the world. I think it has helped people from both positions to listen to what others say and to realize that in both groups there is diversity in how they hold and apply their positions. People have realized that the "other side" is also looking to Scripture for guidance not, as too often in the past, assuming they know what the "other side" believes and why it is unbiblical.

Lis: What was fascinating for us as authors was the response to the book. Reviews commented as much about *how* we had written as about *what* we had written. There is no doubt that people were hungry for the subject matter – we have both been kept busy speaking about this subject ever since – but we have also been asked constantly about the *way* we wrote. The reviews kept coming back to this:

> *Most importantly, despite the fact that they disagree with one another, and are able to clearly outline why, they manage to keep the whole discussion friendly, positive, and within the appropriate context of the fact that it's okay to agree to disagree…* [2]

> *… what stands out is the tone of the debate which is friendly. The emails show a concern for one another and prayer for the different things go[ing] on in their lives at the time of writing the book. I believe this tone makes the reader take seriously the more serious arguments that they have… If this book had come out years ago, we might have had better debates. It will foster mutual respect and encourage people to come to their own conclusions based on biblical evidence.* [3]

Both have a deep love of the Bible and their conversation with each other is respectful, robust and profound. The emails are set in the context of the realities of their lives and the intersection of family, work and personal concerns with the theological issues they are wrestling with. This is not a dry academic debate; it is rooted in the identity and passion of two women wanting to serve God to the best of their ability, being true to what they believe God is calling them to in his word.[4]

As Anne Dyer said in the foreword, "This book contains a model of theological discourse from which many – men as well as women – can learn."[5]

As the subject of "good disagreement" has moved further up the agenda, we have found more and more people talking to us about our experience. Has it changed anything? There is no doubt that it has. It has opened doors to discussion which were not open before, between people and groups who previously were just not talking. Serious and important conversations have been possible between AWESOME (the group we are both involved in for ordained evangelical women in the Church of England) and Reform (a group within the Church of England which is generally conservative on women's roles).[6] Relationships have been forged across what previously felt, in many cases, like an uncrossable divide and real friendships have been built between evangelical ordained women and their more conservative counterparts.[7]

Practising good disagreement

Clare: Lis and I clearly disagree on what women can and can't do within ministry and the family. The opportunity to engage in debate on this issue was not something we sought, and this helped us in the way we engaged with each other, because we weren't trying to champion our pet cause. I think that while this subject is important, it is a "second order" issue. In other words, we can hold differing views and not undermine the gospel. I can support and encourage my brothers and sisters in Christ who hold a different view on women's ministry and work alongside them in ways that I wouldn't be able to do if I felt that they clearly undermined the gospel by what they taught or how they lived.

Holding my complementarian position does have implications for how I can work with others holding the egalitarian position. I have happily gone to inductions of female friends becoming vicars because, while we disagree on whether a woman should head up a local church, I can see how they might have reached their decision from Scripture and at one level I want to see them flourishing in gospel ministry. However, a few years ago I was asked by two friends to preach in their churches. Initially I said yes to both, but as I reflected on what I believed about headship and preaching I had to say no to one of them (although I did offer my help in other ways if needed). The difference was that one was a man and the other was a woman. The preaching and teaching ministry within a local church is an area, I believe, where authority and headship is seen. I reached the conclusion that I can preach from time to time, in a way that does not undermine that principle, if it is clear that it is done under the authority of the male vicar and on a more occasional basis.

Lis: As we engaged with the Scriptures together and worked hard at the tough issues, we found that it transformed us. Neither of us changed our minds, but I think we came to understand ourselves and each other better. It is good to ask whether this is different from other subjects and other contentious issues which we as Christians face together. On one level it is no different, as the mandate to seek unity and relationship always holds. On another level, every new issue we face is different because the layout of the ground is different. As we step out of our castles to talk, there are always questions about what is at stake: Are the discussions really concerned with the flourishing of the other, seeking the likeness of Christ in all, or just with getting our own way? Are we genuinely meeting on the same terms, being honest with each other and faithful to Scripture? Will the terms of any agreement be kept? In conversations over women bishops, I sat with people who had no concern for those who disagreed with them and were quite clear that any compromises were temporary and that the long-term game plan was to get them out of the church. Then the disagreement, rather than seeking the other's good, becomes dishonest and destructive.

As we face new realities, we need to be clear what our baselines are, where we stand as we talk, how we disagree. Clare and I were able to come out of our castles and know the Bible was, for both of us, the central, key authority on which we built everything else. We therefore also knew that we wouldn't stop at the theology of experience but needed to allow God's revelation of himself to speak into our experiences, to challenge them, and to open them up to his Spirit and his word. If that priority is not held in common, then the ground shifts.

Clare: I would find it hard to work closely with someone whose teaching I believed to be unbiblical on central issues, such as denying the atonement, or undermining the uniqueness and divinity of Christ, or adopting a lifestyle rejected by Scripture. I could not in all good conscience say "That's fine. You believe that and I will believe this, and it's all OK", if it was something that undermined the gospel. Equally, it would be hard to work closely with someone who did not take the authority of Scripture seriously. In many ways I am still working out the day-to-day implications of how I relate to those people as different situations arise. In a local context it may mean a willingness to attend the same clergy meetings but not be involved in any joint mission initiatives.

But even where we cannot "agree to disagree" the way we disagree still needs to be gracious and loving. To paint it in extreme terms, the Bible says we are to love our enemies (Luke 6:35), so even more should we love those who claim to be brothers and sisters in Christ. We should seek to engage with them and to listen to them (not assume we know exactly what they think and believe). We should go with them to the Bible and see what it has to say on the issue and above all be praying for them. The difficulty arises, of course, when the person we are trying to debate with has a different starting point, not sitting under the authority of Scripture.

What has come across so clearly is the importance of respect and humility as we talk, building up the relationship rather than just winning the argument. Paul in teaching about unity in the body of Christ urges us to "make every effort to keep the unity of the Spirit through the bond of peace" (Ephesians 4:3; NIV), going on to tell us to speak the truth in love (Ephesians 4:15). All too often we are more concerned about winning the argument than seeking unity and peace.

It is much easier to stay in our groups where people around us agree with what we believe, rather than being made to think and to struggle by listening to and engaging with others' views. But staying in our cliques, not being willing to engage with different viewpoints, does not promote unity and a sense of partnership in the gospel. It smacks more of arrogance and a lack of the humility in which we are to consider others better than ourselves (Philippians 2:1–4). That is not to say that we mustn't stand firm on what we believe the Bible teaches. It does not mean that by engaging with someone else's viewpoint we are necessarily condoning it. But we do always need to be going back to the Bible and asking the Holy Spirit to help us in our understanding of it. We need to be willing, if we are mistaken (after all, we are human and sinful), to change our position. There will be times when we have to take a stand and speak out when what someone says undermines the gospel, or their lifestyle brings disrepute to God's church. This can be very costly and should never be done lightly. We need always to ask God to make sure the plank is out of our eye first (Matthew 7:3–5) and to be humble and gracious.

Lis: Good disagreement is not an optional extra for the Christian. It is a gospel mandate. No matter what we disagree about, or with whom we disagree, we must do it in a godly way. We cannot be those who disagree judgmentally or using foghorns. We have been commanded not to judge because we will be judged with the same measure with which we judge others (Matthew 7:1–2). It is so easy to fling print at each other rather than get to know one another and build relationships. I have too often been asked to sign a statement of protest when it would be better to sit round a table.

We are called to be agents of reconciliation, acknowledging that "God was in Christ reconciling the world to himself" (2 Corinthians 5:19) and that he has committed to us this message of reconciliation. This message is about the good news of the cross and we are called to be agents of this reconciliation first and foremost, but we cannot do this if we live in a way that breeds conflict within Christ's body, the church. There will be times when good disagreement means not just that we disagree, but also that we are in very different places and that we think the other is profoundly wrong. I have on several occasions found myself having to say, when working with colleagues on committees, that I disagree with them profoundly and have to distance myself from decisions and actions they have made. If I am honest, I anticipate that there will be more occasions in the future when this will happen.

For me the big issue is when our disagreement goes to the heart of our doctrine, when it challenges our understanding of God, of what it means to be human made in his image and therefore what it means to have a world-changing gospel of redemption. This is very hard because challenging another brother or sister in Christ is not an easy thing to do, but it is something which, if we are to be faithful, we have to do, and it is something which is best done from a place of relationship. I believe that we should constantly reach out, constantly strive for reconciliation, as God does with us. But reconciliation is not soft, it does not acquiesce when things are wrong; it challenges and speaks the truth in love (Ephesians 4:15), it walks the way of the cross. If we don't strive, even at great cost, for unity then those to whom we preach will not know that we are Christ's disciples and they will not know that he was sent by the Father.

***

Questions

1. Do you have a friendship with a fellow Christian with whom you strongly disagree, similar to the situation described in this chapter? How does your friendship change your approach to the disagreement?

2. Why do conversations like this often lead to criticism from fellow Christians (on both sides)? How should we respond to such critiques?

3. How important is prior agreement that "our baseline had to be Scripture" if there is to be "good disagreement"? What changes when this foundation is not in place?

4. From this chapter, and your own experience, what virtues and spiritual disciplines are necessary for there to be "good disagreement"? How do we cultivate these in the church?

5. Are there places of disagreement where you need to move from a castle to a conversation with other Christians? How in the light of this chapter can you go about doing this?

9

Ministry in Samaria: Peacemaking at Truro Church

Tory Baucum

Truro Anglican Church is a large charismatic congregation in Fairfax, near Washington, DC. In 2006 it separated from the Episcopal Church and is now part of the Anglican Church in North America, a parallel and more theologically conservative province. The separation came in the midst of acrimonious disagreements and led to lengthy litigation with the Episcopal Diocese of Virginia, which claimed control of Truro's property. But under its new rector, Tory Baucum, the congregation has pioneered bridge-building with former enemies, both inside and outside the church. This chapter, an extended reflection upon Jesus' mission to the Samaritan woman at the well, is an apologia for Truro's peacemaking ministry.

Introduction

Truro parish sits on the border of the northern and southern parts of the United States, thirteen miles south of the nation's capital. Its geographic setting has undoubtedly influenced its history of peacemaking, often amidst seismic national conflict. Our congregation has found itself positioned between warring parties, learning to follow Jesus between the proverbial "rock and a hard place". In recent years, our discipleship has taken particular inspiration from Jesus' interaction with the Samaritan woman in

John chapter 4. This is a timely biblical tradition because Truro has had several "Samaritan moments" in its history. For example, the first land skirmish of the Civil War happened on our front lawn, at the corner of North Street and Main Street in Fairfax. When the first Confederate soldier killed in the war was shot a stone's throw from Truro (then Zion Church), his body was brought into the parlour of Mr and Mrs Thomas Moore. Perhaps they helped add reconciliation to Truro's DNA, as Mrs Moore was from New York, married to a Virginia Confederate. It was noteworthy that Thomas Moore was a member of Truro and a faithful Episcopalian, although Anglicans had put his grandfather Jeremiah in jail in Alexandria, near Washington, DC, for "preaching the gospel without a license" (that is, planting the First Baptist Church in Alexandria). Jeremiah had been an Episcopal lay reader but had a conversion experience at a Baptist meeting (something normally frowned upon). Jailed yet undeterred, he preached to his congregants through the window. Thomas Jefferson spoke out in his defence and later codified a legal solution into the Virginia constitution.

Unlike Jeremiah Moore I am conflict adverse. But I am not conflict avoidant. In part because God is teaching us that the road to reconciliation – the art of peacemaking – passes through, not around, conflict. Furthermore, the path of peace is a biblical and ecclesial trodden path. And it is one we are learning to walk with Jesus as we take the whole Bible more seriously, learning to read the various parts in terms of the whole symphony of biblical revelation and its reception in the history of the church. As such, this chapter is both a witness to our peacemaking and the biblical hermeneutic that powers and informs it. It accords well with what Matthew Levering calls "participatory exegesis", a mode of biblical interpretation that is founded on three steps:

Reclaiming history as a participatory rather than merely linear reality; understanding biblical exegesis as an ecclesial participation in God the Teacher; and renewing our sense of how the Church's wisdom-

practices… distinguish multilayered and embodied exegesis from the idolatrous distortions of eisegesis.[1]

It illustrates how we are learning to read one part (John 4) in terms of the whole (Genesis to Revelation) – a narrative arc that begins and ends with a wedding in a garden – with an eye towards missionary engagement. Specifically, it is an attempt to understand Jesus' journey to the Samaritan – the "poster child" heretic of his day – in terms of the nuptial character of the Christian mission throughout history.

The Jews of Jesus' day normally went around Samaria, rather than through it. John bluntly reminds the reader of the reason for the Samaritan woman's cool encounter with Jesus: "For Jews have no dealings with Samaritans" (John 4:9; ESV). A cursory reading of the Old Testament reveals that Jesus and the woman at the well inherited a chequered history. Their respective ancestors from the northern and southern tribes of Israel were characterized by taking advantage of the other's alternating vulnerabilities. Occasionally they would show mercy to each other, but that was the exception rather than the rule. Jesus crafted his memorable parable of the good Samaritan around one of those exceptions in salvation history (see 2 Chronicles 28:8–15 and Luke 10:25–37), in which Jesus teaches his disciples (including us) how to faithfully navigate their own complex history in order to engage "the other".

There are other reasons Jews avoided Samaritans. Most important among them, Samaritans had intermarried pagans during the Assyrian and Babylonian exiles. Outside of Israel Samaritans were seen as Jews. But inside the boundaries of Israel they were viewed at best as apostate Jews and at worst as out-and-out pagans.[2] They were the quintessential "heretics" of Jesus' day. And there were good reasons for seeing them so. Samaritans effectively altered the three pillars of Jewish faith and practice. They customized their own:

1. Torah – Samaritan Pentateuch edited according to Samaritan ideology

2. Temple – Gerizim vs Jerusalem as the site of divine encounter

3. Territory – Samaria vs Judah as the privileged land of promise.

Jesus and the Samaritan woman carried this history into their encounter, and it seriously impeded their ability to communicate and relate to one another. Despite this difficulty, it is fascinating to look at how Jesus affirms yet also critiques each of these Jewish-cum-Samaritan pillars. In other words, Jesus does not treat the Samaritan woman as though she is living in a complete zone of darkness, devoid of God's revelation and grace. Rather he enters her *Territory* as part of God's good (but damaged) creation. He then discusses the *Temple* and suggests it has fulfilled its purpose in salvation history (which he had prophetically portrayed in John 2). He quotes and embodies the *Torah* in his own life and work (both in John 4 and throughout the entirety of the Gospel). We witness both affirmation and critique in Jesus' encounter with the woman. Despite this divisive history characterized by severe religious disputes, none of which Jesus papers over, they still share much in common. Jesus the peacemaker seeks to discover and traverse those commonalities. Jesus demonstrates that adversaries require common ground in order to overcome enmity; that there is an underlying unity greater and more powerful than the conflict. And he is that unity.

We will explore this greater unity in the three moments of peace that lead to reconciliation. We will take them in the order they occur in our story. Each moment centres upon an image or sign that points beyond itself to the greater reality of reconciliation. The logic of these images of peace – gift, reciprocity, and fruitfulness – is, in fact, the logic of the gospel. As revealed in John's nuptial drama, they help orient both the church's interpretation of the text and its ongoing interaction with past and modern day "Samaritans". This Samaritan history is not simply prologue. It's not even past. It is a very real and present opportunity for mission. And mission follows the pathway of peace.[3]

First moment: At the well – peace as gift

There is much more happening in John 4 than an intra-faith or interfaith dialogue. We have before us a classic "well scene", which should trigger the biblical imagination to remember the stories of Isaac, Jacob, and Moses, all of whom wooed women at the well (see Genesis 24, where Abraham's servant acts as Isaac's proxy in wooing Rebekah; Genesis 29; Exodus 2:15–22). The Jewish literary scholar Robert Alter has identified these as "type scenes": whenever a man and woman are at a well, the biblical narrative is priming us to see a nuptial drama.[4] The scenes have four main moments:

1. The man journeys (usually from another region) to a well where he meets a local woman.

2. A conversation ensues, whereupon water is drawn from the well.

3. The woman departs to tell her friends and family about the man she has met.

4. The marriage is consummated, usually after a shared meal.

Three of the four moments clearly appear in John 4, and I will suggest that the fourth also occurs but is elusive and deferred until later in the Gospel. Jesus has already been called "the bridegroom" (John 3:29), raising the question "Who is the bride?"[5]

Given the chequered history between Jews and Samaritans (southerners and northerners respectively), it is remarkable that Jesus goes to Samaria, locates the well of Jacob, sits, and strikes up a conversation with a local woman. It is the longest and most detailed narrative of symbolic betrothal in the Bible (excluding, possibly, the Book of Revelation). And, surprisingly, the bride is personified as the most ineligible of brides: a Samaritan who has a most unpromising résumé when it comes to marriage. She is clearly "damaged goods". One could even say she is "Samaria incarnate", divorced from her covenantal people and excluded in shame. Samaria itself is embodied in her multiple alienations.

So we see that the story not only sets up an ethnic and religious barrier (a Samaritan) but also a moral one (a multiple-divorcée). It would seem this is a clear case of "three strikes and you are out". But not so with Jesus. John gives the most extensive portrayal of a marriage proposal to the least likely marriage prospect. This is consistent with John's use of signs: they are both elusive and paradoxical. These signs make you pause and reflect on what is really being said. There is always more here than meets the eye – both within John's narrative and with Jesus.

So what is the nature of the betrothal in John 4? The betrothal at stake is a spiritual one. It is an invitation into the new covenant, which transcends all marriage but to which marriage itself points and in some mysterious manner participates (see Ephesians 5:21–33). It is that which the prophets of Israel promised: the time when the Lord purifies his people from idolatry and betroths her to himself. Hosea, a prophet from the Northern Kingdom of Samaria, spoke:

> *And in that day, declares the* LORD, *you will call me "My Husband",*
> *and no longer will you call me, "My Baal". For I will remove the*
> *names of the Baals from her mouth, and they shall be remembered by*
> *name no more… And I will betroth you to me forever; I will betroth*
> *you to me in righteousness and in justice, in steadfast love and in mercy.*
> *I will betroth you to me in faithfulness. And you shall know the* LORD.
> *(Hosea 2:16–17, 19–20;* ESV*)*

The "now" that Jesus speaks to the woman is the (partial) fulfilment of this promise of Hosea: "But the hour is coming and is *now* here, when the true worshippers will worship the Father in Spirit and truth, for the Father is seeking such people to worship him" (John 4:23; ESV). But John gives us more than the "what" of reconciliation. He actually portrays the means of reconciliation. Jesus is not only the truth the woman seeks but also the grace of how to receive the truth.

This should not surprise us. In John's prologue, Jesus is portrayed as both God's grace and his truth. In the work of peacemaking, grace and truth are not opposed. Especially if we follow the biblical order: grace *before* truth (John 1:14). We see that order on display in this betrothal scene. Jesus woos her, slowly and gently revealing the truth about each other. Jesus does not overpower her. Any biblically informed notion of sovereignty will never violate God's nature of loving respect for his bride. In other words, God does not overpower us with the truth. He gently and kindly woos us.

So Jesus, God incarnate, goes to Samaria and sits at Jacob's Well. Then Samaria incarnate – divorced and estranged from her covenanted people – sits next to him. What does the well represent? A common history? Yes. A common ancestor? That, too. Jacob is a patriarch of both Judah and Israel, of both Jews and Samaritans. Indeed the well is located in the land of Samaria, which historically was the land of the Northern Kingdom, Israel. It is a natural bridge between an estranged people – and given the well's role in previous nuptial dramas, Jesus deliberately chooses that location to reach across the divide.

ST FRANCIS IN DAMIETTA: THIRTEENTH-CENTURY SAMARIA

There are numerous "Jacob's Wells" in the history of the church – meeting places where warring sides attempt to make peace. One of the most important occurred during the fifth Crusade. In the autumn of 1219, Francis of Assisi travelled to Damietta in Egypt to share the gospel with the Sultan al-Kamal.[6] Based on the slender evidence available, it seems that Francis disapproved of the Crusade but used it as an opportunity to wage another kind of warfare against Islam. He went with the crusading soldiers to Egypt but without sword or shield. He fought differently. He sought common ground with the sultan as a beginning point, not an end, and he used it to proclaim the message of salvation. A great biographer of Francis captures this historic moment in Francis's interior dialogue:

> *What can we do to strengthen the columns of the Church? We cannot fight against the Saracens because we have no arms. Furthermore, what would be gained by fighting? We cannot fight the heretics because we lack dialectic reasoning and intellectual preparation. All we can offer are the arms of the insignificant, that is: love, poverty and peace. What can we do to serve the Church? Only this: to live literally by the Gospel of the Lord.*[7]

The sultan was intrigued by Francis and engaged him in dialogue for a few days. He was drawn to Francis's sincerity and holiness. Unconvinced and unconverted, the sultan released Francis and the brothers who accompanied him unharmed. Francis clearly saw Muslims as religious heretics who should convert, but he also loved them enough to risk his life to proclaim the gospel to them in person. Damietta was thirteenth-century Samaria, and the "Saracens" were thirteenth-century Samaritans. Francis participated, consciously or not, in Jesus' mission to woo them by reaching out in peace.

THE TENTH ANNIVERSARY OF 9/11 AND TRURO'S "SAMARITAN MOMENT"

The 9/11 terrorist attacks in 2001 were not "theoretical" for our congregation. One of the hijacked planes ploughed into the Pentagon, where a number of our parishioners worked. Though no Truro member lost their life in the attack, we did lose friends. So when I was approached to host a peacemaking meeting for the tenth anniversary of the attacks, I brought it before the whole vestry for discernment. After much prayerful deliberation, we decided to accept the invitation and partnered with Calvin College and the Berkley Center and hosted an evening conversation with Christians, Jews, and Muslims. Each religion had a representative explain the resources of peace in their traditions. Then they took the next step of explaining how their respective traditions are often co-opted for intolerance and even violence.[8]

The structure, which we helped shape, was familiar. We situated the talks and conversation around a meal, much like we do every Friday night in our Alpha course. Truro knows how to do "hospitality-based evangelism". And just as we often experience in Alpha, we made friends for Jesus by being friends. In the process, we became friends with local Muslims, a friendship that continues with the local Turkish mosque. Just as on Alpha, we did not paper over differences but instead we provided a venue – a "Jacob's Well" – where commonalities and differences could be explored and discussed in the context of affection and respect.

Friendship has surprises. The following year members of the mosque studied the book of Romans with us, attending a weekend conference with Bible scholar Ben Witherington. The court trial that determined ownership of church property went through several iterations. When we lost the third and final court case in 2012, one of the first calls I received was from Bilal Ankaya, the local imam, inviting us to share his mosque. When I shared the news with the congregation, there was an audible gasp of surprise followed by applause. So what are we learning? Peacemaking begins with the gift you make of yourself to the other. It is a liminal – a boundary crossing – experience where room for dialogue is made at the expense of retaliation. Finding a "well" of common humanity and shared history is the pathway to peace.

Second moment: Conversing over water – peace as reciprocity

All reconciled people begin by finding common ground. But what if something we thought was common turns out, on closer inspection, to be part of the division? For example, some claim that Christians and Muslims worship the same God, but what if our understanding of God is so different that under closer scrutiny this proposition is shown to be untrue? As monotheists, we both say we believe in one God, but Christians also believe in Jesus as the eternal Son of the Father, so to what extent is our agreement in "the unity of God" meaningful? We won't know the answer to that question unless we begin a conversation, a dialogue to clarify our terms and premises.[9]

Jesus and the Samaritan woman found something in common – a common design as male and female, bridegroom and bride – at Jacob's Well. But what brought them to the well was not merely their common history. There was more. They shared a common desire: they thirsted. Just as Jesus initiates problematic contact at the well, he initiates a conversation that is laced with misunderstanding and danger. We see both in the woman's response to his request for a drink: "How is it that you, a Jew, ask for a drink from me, a woman of Samaria?" (John 4:9; ESV). In this one gesture Jesus throws a bridge over two chasms simultaneously:

- The religious chasm that existed between the Jew and the Samaritan, the orthodox and the heterodox, the devout and the deviant believer. In this chasm, Jesus inserts three moments of truth: true desire, true confession, and true revelation. Each moment of truth progressively leads to the next.

- The gender chasm that existed between men and women since the Fall. Here we come to the fourth and final moment of truth: the goal of true peacemaking (which will be discussed under the "Third moment" below).

Jesus' request for water is really a humble invitation that makes the conversation possible. With these words "Give me a drink", he is putting himself in the position of a recipient. He is asking the woman for help and, by doing so, he is restoring her agency. Much like when Jesus commandeered Peter's boat and transformed it into a pulpit for the crowds that had pressed upon him on the shore of Galilee (Luke 5:1–11), Jesus again takes the humble way with a would-be disciple. He says to someone who does not yet believe "Will you help me?" Humility is a proven pathway to receptivity. And without receptivity there is no reciprocity. Antagonists remain frozen in their own moral sterility.

The first "moment of truth" is true desire. Jesus ups the ante and offers the woman "living water", so we begin to see that the water in the well is an object lesson for something greater. This offer initiates the substantial bulk of their dialogue and points to their common desire. Jesus is not referring to water from a different source but an altogether different kind of water – water that can be had without a ladle. This is a critical moment in the conversation, for Jesus reveals his desire to give her life. Noticing Jesus' paradoxical behaviour, Augustine of Hippo asks, "The One who asked to drink is indeed the giver of water. Why did He ask to drink, then?" Augustine's answer: Jesus was thirsty indeed – but thirsty more for the woman's faith than her water. He was thirsty for quenching her thirst, through the gradual revelation of himself. He continues, "His 'drink' was to do the will of him that sent him. That was why he said, 'I thirst; give me to drink', namely, to work faith in her and to drink of her faith and transplant her into his body, for his body is the church." [10]

The second "moment of truth" is true confession. Jesus tells her to bring her husband. She says she has no husband, which is accurate but not the whole truth. Jesus, still in wooing mode, challenges her to be more transparent and supplies the left-out information that she has had five husbands and her current partner is not her husband (John 4:18). So she has had six men and the seventh man – the perfect man – is now wooing her. Jesus does not ignore her disordered and sinful lifestyle, but pinpoints it and calls her to something better. Here the nuptial nature of this drama is made explicit. She is ineligible for marriage in the natural order (which hasn't worked out very well for her), but she is highly eligible for the marriage Jesus is proposing.

This brings us to the third "moment of truth", true revelation – the truth about Jesus' own identity. All through the narrative there has been a "growth in Christology", as the woman slowly begins to see who Jesus really is. [11] First she calls him "a Jew" (verse 9), then the more neutral "Sir" (verses 11, 15), then "a prophet" (verse 19). Finally she says, "I know that Messiah is coming (he who is called

Christ). When he comes he will tell us all things", and Jesus replies, "I who speak to you am he" (verses 25–26). Some scholars believe this is the first of several "*ego eimi*" ("I am") sayings in John's Gospel, a formulation which indicates the personal presence of God. The woman has kept Jesus, through various titles – Jew, Sir, Prophet, and Messiah – at a distance. Each title preserves a safe I–It, subject–object relationship. But with this final and most personal revelation of Jesus they now have the potential for an I–Thou, subject-to-subject, person-to-person, relationship.

What Jesus models throughout this whole conversation – allowing himself to be named, gradually revealing the true nature of his interlocutor, and slowly unveiling his own identity – is the reciprocity of betrothal. There is a faithful exchange of ideals and desires, however tentative at first, leading to insight and trust, which results in revelation. What do we learn from this exchange? The way out of relationship is also the way back in. When trust has been broken so has relationship. Jesus restores the relationship by first restoring the trust! This is the logic of reconciliation: trust is restored before relationship. It is a most precious and fragile moment of peacemaking. And in this moment we begin to see its true nature. Peacemaking is neither making nice nor even the cohabitation of differences. That is cheap and essentially pagan behaviour (see Matthew 5:46–47). Biblical peacemaking, on the other hand, is giving life, restoring relationship, to our adversary.

ST FRANCIS DE SALES IN GENEVA: SEVENTEENTH-CENTURY SAMARIA

There are notable moments when the church was as divided and estranged as the Jews and the Samaritans and as Jesus was with the Samaritan woman. And there are many examples of Christian disagreement that split the church at its deepest levels. But there are also notable exceptions and counter pressures. There are those moments when Christian leaders, inspired and inhabited by Jesus, follow the path of reciprocity – of a kind of dialogue that demonstrates both grace and truth and, most importantly, grace before truth.

St Francis shows us the way – the way of building a bridge of grace that bears the weight of truth. This time it is not St Francis of Assisi, but rather St Francis de Sales, missionary Bishop of Geneva from 1602, who models this second moment of peace. De Sales was banned from his episcopal see city, as were all Roman Catholics, yet he made several forays into Geneva to meet and converse with Theodore Beza, John Calvin's successor. Beza was a major Reformed theologian, widely reviled in Roman Catholic circles, and senior to de Sales by almost half a century. What made de Sales able to meet with this Protestant "heretic" and, more importantly, what steeled him to stand against the adverse opinion of his own church when he did so? We need to make a quick foray into the Wars of Religion to answer that question, but it is worth the detour.

The seventeenth century was the hinge century between the medieval and modern worlds, a time of great violence motivated especially by religious intolerance arising both from the Reformation and the Counter-Reformation. Two modern fixtures came from this century of religious feuding – the Enlightenment and ecumenical peacemaking. The former was exemplified by René Descartes and his programme of doubt; the latter by Francis de Sales and his programme of love. Both were responses to the Wars of Religion. Descartes sought to insulate society from religiously motivated violence by annexing all of its truth claims to the realm of private opinion. As a mathematician, he made use of mathematical precision and public demonstration as a criterion for truth claims. De Sales also sought to insulate society from religious violence but by changing the heart of religious opponents toward each other. Obviously, we Westerners are much more the children of Descartes than we are of de Sales. Most of us are Cartesians; few are Salesians.

In his first sermon as a missionary priest in Geneva, de Sales pledged himself to a strategy of love:

The walls of Geneva must be broken down by charity and it is by charity that we must invade this city and recover it... Let our camp not be one of war but let it be God's camp where the trumpets ring out loud and clear: Holy, holy, holy is the Lord of Hosts... It is by our own hunger and thirst, not by that of a beleaguered enemy that we must repel our adversaries.[12]

When de Sales became bishop he augmented his strategy of love with two tactics. First, he would only ordain priests he was convinced loved Protestants. Second, in discussions with Protestants he would only use the authorities they believed in. Thus he argued only from Scripture and the Church Fathers, never from Thomist scholasticism. But his chief strategy was always to love the opponent. He wrote: "Whoever preaches with love preaches adequately against heretics, even if he doesn't bring out a single word of argument directed against them."[13] His confidence in the love of God – the love which creates and sustains the world, and above all honours everybody's free choice to love or refuse love – was the driving motive for reaching out to Theodore Beza. In one of their meetings, de Sales asked Beza if he believed Roman Catholics could be saved. Beza, after a fifteen-minute pause, answered, "Yes, I do."[14] Their relationship moved haltingly from I–It to I–Thou. They began to engage each other as estranged brothers rather than merely ecclesiastical opponents. Several times de Sales entered Geneva, at the risk of his own life, to talk to the ageing reformer. What motivated him to befriend and woo the heart of Beza? And just as important, what motivated him to stand nearly alone in the Roman Catholic hierarchy as a friend of Protestants? It was the path of peace which leads to unity and not merely to cohabit with differences.

BEFRIENDING AN EPISCOPAL BISHOP

In March 2011 I finally made the drive to Richmond, Virginia, to meet the Episcopal bishop, Shannon Johnston. The meeting was tentative at first. It warmed slightly when I gave him a copy of poetry by Adam Zagajewski.[15] By the end of the meeting Shannon suggested we meet monthly to pray, with no other agenda. I agreed.

Two weeks later his chancellor, Russ Palmore, died suddenly, unexpectedly and, for Shannon, tragically. I and other leaders of Truro attended the funeral in Richmond. I patted his shoulder on my way out of the church, but we did not speak. Since we had already scheduled our second meeting in order to pray, we met two weeks after the funeral. He spent the first twenty minutes expressing his grief over Russ's unexpected death. And he took almost as much time expressing gratitude for Truro's graciousness in attending the funeral. The meeting lasted over two hours. I remember thinking to myself on the drive back to Fairfax: "I not only like this guy but I think we are going to become friends. This is really weird." Throughout the rest of the year we maintained our monthly prayer meetings. At the suggestion of my daughter, Isabelle, we started to augment these with conversation over a beer across the street at the Jefferson Hotel. What started as an I–It caricatured relationship between liberal bishop and conservative rector became an I–Thou relationship of trust and affection. In short, adversaries became friends.

In January 2012 Truro lost the third and final round of litigation against the Episcopal diocese. The next Sunday my friend Canon Andrew White, the "Vicar of Baghdad", preached to a packed house. The night before he had been with Shannon at a ceremony in Richmond where he was awarded the International First Freedom Award. He began the sermon by explaining his credentials to speak on conflict and peace: "I have buried 273 of my members in the last two years. I know something of conflict." But after recalling his dinner with Shannon the night before, he surprised me with these words: "The Episcopal bishop wants to work with you simply because your rector has loved him." In April our vestry settled with the Episcopal diocese and shortly afterwards Shannon gave us an eighteen-month rent free lease (it has since been extended). Our friendship became public and very controversial. Shannon's response to the controversy was to clear his calendar and accompany me to the Holy Trinity Brompton leadership conference in London in May 2012, which was followed by an invitation to tell our story at the Faith in Conflict Conference at Coventry Cathedral in February 2013. Even though our witness of peacemaking was vigorously opposed by certain factions within the Anglican Communion, and suffered temporary setbacks, the friendship survived.

What is God teaching us in this moment of peace? Peacemaking extends an I–Thou, nuptial relationship into the field of battle. At its heart, peacemaking is giving life and dignity to your adversary, not simple cohabiting with differences. And dignity follows the pathway of dialogue. This creates the conditions for reconciliation but doesn't guarantee it. For reconciliation to occur one must enter the third moment of peace.[16]

Third moment: The wedding – peace as fruitfulness

I have suggested the encounter at the well and the dialogue around water connects Jesus and the woman at the point of their common design and common desire. This design as male and female and their thirst (yearning desire) have the makings of a nuptial drama. Up to this point our story follows the pattern of an Old Testament type scene. The couple meet and converse at the well. Then the woman leaves to tell her people, and she returns to introduce them to her suitor. She came to the well for drawing water but instead returns to the city full of desire to communicate to others the wonderful news that fills her to overflowing (John 4:14). When Jesus tells the disciples to pray for harvesters for the fields that are already ripe for harvest, perhaps he is inviting prayer for this new disciple who is returning home to tell her friends about the man "who told me everything I ever did" (verse 29). The Samaritan woman is depicted as an evangelist, one who brings others to meet Jesus, just as Andrew and Philip do in John chapter 1.

But if this is a nuptial drama, where is the wedding? Type scenes are inherently flexible, and John's symbolism is both elusive and reflexive. Signs in the first half of the Gospel are fulfilled in the second half, but in such a way that we are forced to reconsider what we read earlier. There is a dialectic between the so-called "book of signs" (chapters 1–12) and the "book of glory" (chapters 13–20), which causes us to reconsider what we thought we already "knew". This dialectic – this looking back and forth between sign and fulfilment in such counter-intuitive ways – is a spiritual pedagogy that induces humility and patience in the disciple, especially as we are recruited into the nuptial mystery of the work of reconciliation. It also keeps us focused on the end, the consummation of our union with our Bridegroom Messiah.

Jesus never got that ladle of water from the woman at the well. In that sense, he remained thirsty until he had finished his Father's work. There is only one other place in John's Gospel where Jesus is thirsty "at the sixth hour" – when he was hanging on the cross: "After this, Jesus, knowing that all was now finished, said (to fulfil the Scripture), 'I thirst'" (John 19:28; ESV). Till the very end Jesus carried his thirst for us, his bride, and gave himself to us in order to quench his desire. The betrothal introduced in chapter 4 is consummated in chapter 19. Jesus' passion is the climactic moment of this entire nuptial drama. This is when he gives his body completely and unreservedly for us, his bride. Augustine extols the nuptial nature of the cross with this unforgettable flourish:

Like a bridegroom Christ went forth from his chamber... he came to the marriage bed of the cross and there mounting it, he consummated his marriage. And when he perceived the sighs of the creature, he lovingly gave himself up to the torment in place of his bride and joined himself to her forever.[17]

In such light we begin to see the work of reconciliation to which we are called. The peacemaking we do to achieve reconciliation is something much more than cohabiting with differences. Rather it is giving life to those with whom we are estranged, resulting in friendship which impacts a wider circle of relationships. This is the goal of peacemaking: restored communion. There is an urgency to invite the lost that supersedes all natural desire and order – even such a fundamental desire as hunger and thirst. Everything takes a back seat to this grand preparation for the marriage supper of the Lamb. This is the communion toward which human history strains and to which preachers of the gospel point. Human history is sandwiched between two weddings (Eden and the New Jerusalem), and, like John the Baptist, we herald the bridegroom's intentions. The prospect of this grand cosmic consummation – symbolized initially by the gesture of untying the sandal strap – is what summons and repairs our repentance (see Ruth 4:7–10; John 1:26–27).

WESLEY'S URBAN MISSION TO ENGLAND: EIGHTEENTH-CENTURY SAMARIA

Who in church history participates in and exemplifies this third moment of peacemaking – the moment of recognizing and wooing the other into her destiny of common discipleship to Jesus? One would be hard pressed to find a better example than the eighteenth-century Anglican clergyman John Wesley. Wesley was nuptial both in his message ("perfect love" as the defining character of Christians) and ministry (eventually ordaining women as ministers in the movement). Regrettably the nuptial nature of early Methodism is often overlooked. This oversight is all the more remarkable given Methodism's romantic nature and genesis in the very class-conscious and masculine age of emerging urbanized, industrialized England. Methodism's nuptial nature precipitated a revolution in aesthetics (just as it prevented a political revolution in society) by rehumanizing and integrating the marginalized populations of the urban poor. A few forgotten facts remind us of Methodism's history, especially concerning the inclusion of women in the movement:

- Women exceeded men by a ratio of two to one in the early Methodist societies and bands.

- These small evangelizing and discipling groups were composed of women and sometimes led by women.

- Women were able and encouraged to speak in these public and mixed gender meetings.

- The criteria for such exhortations were effectiveness and gifting, not gender.

- The line between testimony, exhortation, and preaching was not easily drawn. If one was gifted at the first or second, in principle one could continue the path that led to preaching.[18]

In a letter to Mr John Smith, Wesley stated his rationale for including women in leadership and other modifications to ecclesiastical order:

> *I would inquire, what is the end of all ecclesiastical order? Is it not to bring souls from the power of Satan to God? And to build them up in His fear and love? Order, then, is so far valuable as it answers these ends; and if it answers them not it is worth nothing... Wherever the knowledge and love of God are, true order will not be wanting. But the most apostolical [sic] order where these are not is less than nothing and vanity.*[19]

This sort of quotation from Wesley could be multiplied endlessly. They are normally taken as evidence of his supposed "pragmatism". That is a superficial reading. Rather this is evidence for Wesley's eschatologically driven theology – his thirst for nuptial union with God is the teleological pull which advanced the Wesleyan mission.

Ecclesiastical order possesses a penultimate value in Wesley's hierarchy of goods and must always serve the ultimate value of God's thirst for his bride – the personal knowledge of God's love that transforms people and their communities. Wesley pointed to this often as the chief goal of the Methodist movement. The grand objective was a nuptial life in God experienced as "an intimate, an uninterrupted union with God, a constant communion with the

Father and his Son Jesus Christ, through the Spirit; a continual enjoyment of the Three-One God, and of all the creatures in Him".[20] This nuptial vision created in eighteenth-century urban England an almost unparalleled partnership of the sexes, not seen since Assisi, Galilee, and Eden.

Truro's "Samaria" vision

Since Jeremiah and Thomas Moore's experience of battling for human dignity (which the gospel restores) during the Revolutionary and Civil Wars respectively, Truro has had other "Samaritan moments" of crossing ideological boundaries to bear witness to Jesus. For example, during the Civil Rights movement in the 1950s, though the parish itself was divided about the question, Ed Pritchard, a great lay leader of Truro, crossed a very public and controversial boundary against Virginia segregationists on behalf of African Americans. This fortified him for the equally unpopular stand he took for the charismatic movement in the 1970s. No force in American history has been as racially integrating and healing as that of the Pentecostal/charismatic renewal of the church. Truro would not be the Truro it is today if Ed Pritchard had not taken both journeys into "Samaria". With the advent of the charismatic movement, the parish began to experience what the Civil War and Civil Rights movements could never accomplish. Truro began to integrate, not from legislative mandate but from a freeing of the heart by the Holy Spirit.[21] Why do I begin and end this chapter with Truro's long history of making peace? In part, to put the parish's current journey in "Samaria" into its larger participatory history. Truro has a time-tested tradition of crossing the border into Samaria; our historic campus is a virtual "Jacob's Well" of peacemaking.

In 2008 we discerned a new vision statement for our parish: "Radical Hospitality". We believed it was a provisional statement, something God would use to prepare us for the more radical and long-term plans he had for us. Shortly before the publication of that statement, a couple approached us about providing a meeting place for homeless worshippers. It started in their home but outgrew it and they needed both a regular place to meet and help feeding the numbers who attended, often over 100. Truro's vestry discerned God was inviting us to live this vision we had claimed came from him. Hosting and ministering with a homeless congregation is certainly "radical hospitality". Over the next six years, our congregation cooked hundreds of meals, drove vans full of homeless seekers to the service, prayed for them and with them in healing prayer, and even joined the local Coptic church in opening a medical clinic for their care. We made room in our midst because God made room in our hearts. During that time we lost ownership of our building and though we are still residing there, we believe our homeless brothers and sisters taught us to hold our property lightly. They taught us that our spiritual home transcends these beautiful colonial brick buildings and that we can continue to thrive without them.

Now we are concluding a discernment process around a new vision. This vision is likely to be intergenerational in reach and will take Truro through much of the twenty-first century. We believe God is calling us to a renewed commitment to love as he loves: Freely (Gift), Fully (Reciprocity), and Fruitfully. This is the love that creates new life. It is also the love that turns adversaries into friends. It is God's nuptial love. Just as the provisional vision statement of 2008 opened doors, new opportunities have come to us that appear to be God's invitation to step into this vision. Along with a dear Roman Catholic mentor, Don Renzo Bonetti, we have been invited to speak at the World Meeting of the Family (WMF) in Philadelphia on "Rebuilding the Domestic Church". Follow-up ecumenical conferences are already scheduled for subsequent years. The first will be hosted by none other than First Baptist Church, Alexandria, the very same congregation founded by Jeremiah Moore in 1803. The second conference will be hosted by the Roman Catholic diocese of Harrisburg, a historic Roman Catholic diocese in the United States. The invitation to the WMF is a door of opportunity that has already issued into a precious ecumenical moment for our parish. We are becoming a sort of "Taizé of Families" as Catholic and Protestant families come to our parish to learn how to be healed as families and to rebuild the church out of a renewed understanding of nuptial love.

Another door of opportunity to "learn to love like God" is that our former adversaries – principally Muslims and liberal Episcopalians – are becoming friends. We are relearning that peacemaking is not only an imperative of the gospel but it is a principal "plausibility structure", which makes it credible to a doubting world. We are no longer a church at war with others, even though our commitment to orthodoxy is stronger and our standards of holiness are higher than during our days of division. We are not a church that simply wishes to cohabit with differences. Instead we are a church that seeks to give life to our adversaries just as we do to our family and friends. The same gospel that teaches us marriage is the union of husband and wife in the bond of Christ's love also teaches us to be peacemakers.

So what is God teaching us? Peacemaking is both the principal discipline and fruit of a nuptial life. And since nuptiality – a life of union with God and one another that heals creation – is at the heart of the gospel, to not seek peace is to falsify the gospel. Peacemaking does not always lead to reconciliation in our lifetime but without peacemaking we are condemned to a life of sterile judgment and death.

A commonplace of Civil War lore is that when the military conflict ended Northerners complained of Abraham Lincoln's overall leniency toward Southern officers. Union officials demanded he destroy the Confederate enemies – not befriend them. Lincoln responded, "Have I not destroyed my enemy when I have made him my friend?" This is Truro's experience of peacemaking as we participate in a long tradition of "ministry in Samaria".

***

Questions

1. This chapter arises out of the specific history of Truro Church. What in your own history as a Christian or Christian community has shaped your approach to disagreement and peacemaking?

2. From within your Christian tradition, who might be a "Samaritan" you need to make peace with and engage in conversation? How does Jesus' approach in John 4 help?

3. "When trust has been broken so has relationship. Jesus restores the relationship by first restoring the trust!" How do we restore trust when disagreements have led to relationship breakdown?

4. What difference does the offer of "radical hospitality" make to us and to those with whom we disagree?

5. Tory Baucum and Bishop Shannon are still in different churches. How does "good disagreement" enable former adversaries to become friends across the divide?

10

Mediation and the Church's Mission

Stephen Ruttle

Drawing on his long experience as a barrister and now a mediator, Stephen Ruttle here explores how mediation, as a form of peacemaking, can help Christians who disagree and also be a gift to a divided world. After defining mediation and showing its connection with the Christian gospel, he describes the mindset needed to mediate and outlines the structure of a mediation process, before examining its possible outcomes and how it can be a crucial part of the church's own life and mission in the world.

Blessed are the peacemakers

In the Sermon on the Mount, Jesus declares: "Blessed are the peacemakers, for they will be called children of God" (Matthew 5:9; NIV). It is a wonderful promise. God is a peacemaker, and his children share that family likeness, which is recognized by those around them. In the same sermon Jesus gives numerous practical examples of godliness, including the related command: "Love your enemies, and pray for those who persecute you, that you may be children of your Father in heaven" (Matthew 5:44–45; NIV). "Unassisted" peacemaking takes place directly between people when they put this command into action. But sometimes we need help to do so. Mediation, the subject of this chapter, is a form of "assisted" peacemaking. Someone in the middle helps those stuck on either side to try to reach agreement with each other, or at least to disagree as well as possible. Mediation may be needed when the people concerned cannot work things out for themselves. There may be neighbour disputes about noise, rubbish, or boundaries; or community disputes about antisocial behaviour and petty crime, involving the police and the criminal courts. There may be disputes in the workplace, or at school; or between multibillion dollar companies, or married couples; or profound unhealed pain between victims and offenders. The common factor is usually pain. Sometimes this is extreme. Standing in the middle as a mediator is never safe.

But miracles do happen when human beings sit down and talk to each other. Sometimes the outcomes are extraordinary. The opportunities, and the needs, in our secular culture for peacemakers have never been greater. There is an open door for Christians to act as peacemakers in almost every aspect of our increasingly atheistic, post-Christendom, world. We can bring hope where others cannot. A leading Californian mediator who, as far as I am aware, has no overt allegiance to any faith tradition observed recently that the church has the potential to lead the world in this area. The reality, tragically, is rather different. A recent commentator in the secular press, having discussed a contemporary Christian theological dispute, concluded with this inversion of John 13:35: "By this will all men know that you are my disciples, because you loathe each other and despise each other and will not even sit down and talk to each other."

In the light of comments like this, many would now contend that Christians have to earn the right to speak to the world about living in peace. Peter Price, former Bishop of Bath and Wells, observed to me recently: "the greatest missiological theme for this generation is reconciliation". Perhaps then when we act as peacemakers and bridge-builders, when we mediate and stand or sit or weep between people, we are in fact doing mission. Maybe those watching see Someone else present with us.

This chapter assumes that there are profound disagreements between Christians on important issues and that these disagreements are a fact of life which are unlikely to be resolved, at least in the sense that everyone will come to a common viewpoint. The questions that then arise are: How well can we disagree? Can we live together or not? If so, how closely? If not, can we separate with blessing rather than with cursing? Can we love each other despite these disagreements? How well can we "do unity"? This chapter will focus on the mediation phenomenon that has developed very rapidly within the United Kingdom and is spreading worldwide, and encourage readers to see it as a profound gift from God to the church of today and tomorrow.[1]

From barrister to mediator

For nearly twenty-five years I worked as a commercial barrister and then as a Queen's Counsel, much of my time spent in the courtroom. In 1997 I qualified as a commercial mediator, and since 2002 I have been working full time in mediating all types of legal disputes from the very small to the very big. I also set up and continue to help run a community mediation charity (Wandsworth Mediation Service) from our church in Battersea. I work increasingly as a peacemaker within the Church of England (and between faith groups more broadly), mediating, conciliating, and facilitating theological, interpersonal, and congregational disputes. First barrister and now mediator; what is the difference?

As a barrister I was an "on-one-sider".[2] The parties in dispute were, as it were, on opposite sides of the chasm that represented their dispute. I was rooted firmly on one side of this divide. My job was both to advise my client on what I thought were the legal answers to the disagreement and then if necessary to represent the client in court as his or her mouthpiece. The English legal system, which is one of the best in the world, is adversarial. That means that the two parties become involved in a legal battle, which further polarizes them, and the courtroom becomes a warzone. I was fighting on my client's behalf, and my words were the bullets with which I fought.

The judge would decide which party was the winner and which the loser. Winning was good and losing was nasty. Win or lose, however, litigation was never fun; at least not for the clients, who often felt as if they had gone through the mangle.

Mediation is "in-the-middleness", to use Bill Marsh's term. As a mediator, I am an "in-betweener".[3] I am no longer on either side. I stand between people, or groups of people, who are torn apart by unresolved conflict. My role is to help those in dispute to talk to each other and to assist them in finding their own solutions to their disagreements. Words are now building blocks not bullets and the process is bridge-building, rather than winning.

It was primarily because of the major emotional and relational drawbacks of the litigation process, together with its significant costs and delays, that Alternative Dispute Resolution (ADR) initiatives were developed. Mediation of commercial and family disputes began in the United Kingdom in the early 1990s as an import from the United States and is now rapidly spreading throughout Europe and many other jurisdictions across the world. It has succeeded beyond the wildest dreams of those who first promoted it. In 2001 the British government publicly committed to an ADR pledge, and the Lord Chancellor observed that "for most people most of the time litigation should be the method of dispute resolution of last resort". What began as a very alternative process has within twenty years become mainstream civil dispute resolution, and it is here to stay. Most larger cases going through the High Court that have not settled through direct negotiation now mediate; and of those that mediate upwards of 70 per cent settle. A series of recent decisions by the UK courts have strongly supported mediation and have laid down sanctions that apply to parties who do not take it seriously. A quotation from a 2012 Court of Appeal judgment about a neighbour dispute gives a good flavour of the attitude of many judges:

All disputes between neighbours arouse deep passions and entrenched positions are taken as the parties stand on their rights seemingly blissfully unaware or unconcerned that they are committing themselves to unremitting litigation which will leave them bruised by the experience and very much the poorer, win or lose. It depresses me that solicitors cannot at the very first interview persuade their client to put their faith in the hands of an experienced mediator, a dispassionate third party, to guide them to a fair and sensible compromise of an unseemly battle which will otherwise blight their lives for months and months to come… Not all neighbours are from hell. Most simply occupy the land of bigotry. There may be no escape from hell but the boundaries of bigotry can with tact be changed by the cutting edge of reasonableness skilfully applied by a trained mediator. Give and take is often better than all or nothing.[4]

Litigation is all about the outcome; mediation on the other hand is primarily about process, a process that is essentially relational with the mediator standing between two warring parties and helping them to re-engage in order to seek agreement.

Defining mediation

The word "mediator" comes from the late Latin *mediatus* meaning "someone placed in the middle". The *Oxford English Dictionary* definition of mediation is "to intervene for the purpose of reconciling". The *Collins* definition is similar: "to intervene in order to bring about agreement". "In-the-middleness" seems therefore to be an apt description. The mediator does not take a fixed position other than that of being (somewhere) in the middle. In some circles the word "mediation" now presupposes the existence of a legal dispute capable of settlement and, accordingly, involves a commitment by both sides at least to consider the possibility of a final resolution or, on the *OED* meaning, the possibility of reconciliation. But if, as I believe, the only aim is "agreement" (as in the *Collins* definition) then the process is much wider. As we will see, "success" in mediation connotes some form of agreement between the parties. This agreement can be very wide (reconciliation) or very narrow (for instance ceasefire or amicable divorce).

In the past I have encountered opposition to offers of mediation because to one of the parties involved it indicated a commitment in principle to the possibility of reconciliation. That is not as surprising as it might sound. Typically one person might only be prepared to countenance reconciliation if the other person were first to commit to certain prerequisite steps. That other person, however, sees it differently and the process never even gets off the ground. One answer is to define the object of mediation more widely to include the reaching of *any agreement*, however far short of reconciliation. Another answer is to use a different, and perhaps more neutral, term to define the process. *Facilitation* (from the French *facile*) means "to make easier" and in this context contemplates the enabling of more effective conversation. *Conciliation* (from the Latin *conciliare*) means "to assemble, unite, win over" and thus means the bringing together of people perhaps merely into the same room and certainly not necessarily to the same viewpoint. Both terms are thus broader in scope than "mediation", in part because they do not connote the taking up of a middle position between the parties, though of course a good mediator should both facilitate and conciliate. But mediation should not be confused with *arbitration*. Arbitration is a form of judging, albeit in private and usually by a "lay" judge. Mediation does not involve any judgment by the mediator.

What mediation looks like

Let me illustrate the process by reference to a worked demonstration. When speaking on mediation I often invite two members of my audience who know each other to come forward, to face each other and to begin to disagree about a particular issue. That part is rarely difficult! I then ask them to model the typical stages of degeneration of conflict.

At stage 1 they are facing each other, discussing the problem, and learning that they see the issue from quite different perspectives.

This is frustrating. They try harder to persuade each other but get nowhere. Stage 2 starts with them beginning to blame each other for the difficulty. In other words the problem is personalized: "you are the reason for my frustration". This is fertile ground for further frustration, which soon leads to anger. After a while they begin to forget what the problem was really about because they have so much to say about each other. This illustrates the truth that most conflicts have defining issues on the surface but major underlying issues (that may have been there for many years) not far below the surface. Stage 3 begins with increasing hostility and aggression. It ends with one party turning his or her back on the other. This is insulting, and the other follows suit. Stage 4 involves polarization: they physically move apart from each other and at the same time begin to talk to other people about how degenerate the other is. This is called "triangulation". Stage 5 is demonization of the other. They may also by now have mustered their own private armies.

At the end of stage 3 with the parties turning their backs on each other I ask my audience what has just stopped. The answer is "conversation". It may be possible to shout at, and insult, each other with backs turned, but it is not possible to have effective conversation. So what has to happen before such conversation can begin? The answer of course is that both parties have to turn around and face each other. I then enquire how easy or difficult it is to do so. (This is of course a metaphor; would that all conflicts could be resolved by a physical turning around!) The answer is "very difficult", for numerous reasons. At that stage in the conflict the parties are likely to be angry. They may be afraid. They may have suffered huge loss of face. They may have absolutely no idea how to move forward, or lack the emotional resources or vocabulary to deal with their strong feelings. And so they do not turn around. It is much easier either to walk away from each other and never to re-engage, or to begin an assault. These are the classic "flight" and "fight" responses to conflict. Neither works. Those who opt for the flight approach will live thereafter with the realization that the problem was never sorted out, that there was no closure and that they have run away from it. Those who resort to warfare and the intended destruction of their opponent (verbally and sometimes psychologically) will live forever with the consequences.

So how are these people to turn around? Taking the dispute to court does not help. Imagine a triangle. The parties are at the bottom left and the bottom right. At the apex is the judge. For the judge (separated from the parties and sitting above them on the bench) to decide in favour of one against the other may resolve the legal dispute but very rarely restores the broken relationship. The legal process, being adversarial, further polarizes them and pushes them to still further extremes.

Suppose, however, that I cease to model the judge, step down from my bench, and walk towards the parties. I speak to each (still with backs turned and facing away from each other), and with their permission lay a hand on each person's turned shoulder (compare the Old Testament depiction of an umpire or mediator who might "lay his hand on us both", Job 9:33). They feel my hand and turn around to speak to me, but are now facing each other with me in the middle. They are in one sense linked to each other through my stretched arms and also separated from each other by them. Using different metaphors my arms are both bridge (for re-engagement) and buffer (to preserve distance and safety). The visual image of standing with arms outstretched also reminds the audience of the crucifixion. Sometimes indeed mediating feels like being held in position by nails with the parties moving apart and with the mediator increasingly stretched. It may just be the case that the essence of this process, this very in-betweenness itself, is in some way a very pale reflection of what Christ did on the cross. If so, then what we are discussing has profound missional implications.

What do we learn about mediation from this pictorial demonstration?

- Mediation involves an intervention. The mediator moves from distance from the conflict to presence within it; from a position of emotional detachment and safety to a position of danger, at least in emotional terms.

- A relationship is begun between the mediator and each of the parties. The metaphor used to describe the nature of this contact ("laying his hand") is extraordinarily rich and evokes concepts such as compassion, comfort, affirmation, and support. Conflict frequently makes those involved desperate, and deep engagement between parties and mediator can develop very fast.

- A mediator is not a figure of authority like a judge or police officer who can be imposed upon the parties without their consent. This initial agreement by the parties to mediate is significant in itself. It may be the first agreement they have made with each other; granted it is tripartite and with the mediator and not just with each other but it is still an agreement. Its psychological effect is represented in the illustration by them turning around to face the mediator. I sometimes observe to my clients, sitting and spitting at each other around the table, that the very fact they are in the same room means the hardest part of the process has been accomplished.

- The purpose of this shared relationship is not to benefit the mediator. His or her role is merely to act as a link between the parties whereby they may begin to re-engage. As the parties draw together more closely so the mediator backs away until, hopefully, only the parties are left.

- The presence of the in-betweener helps make the process safe. We talk continuously about providing a "safe place" in which some very difficult and painful conversations can take place. In the illustration the outstretched arms, and indeed the very person of the in-betweener, represent a safety barrier. If this means that some of the pain and venom spills over onto the mediator then so be it. Verbal, occasionally physical, blows that would otherwise descend on each other descend instead on the person in the middle.

- The mediator becomes a bridge-builder enabling estranged people not only to "look at" each other, but to begin to re-engage with each other.

What the parties may choose to do thereafter with the bridge that they have been working to establish is a matter for them. The bridge is not necessarily intended to encourage them to leave their fixed positions and migrate across. It is merely a means of access between those living in villages on either side. Those who wish to can meet on it for the purpose of conversation and, possibly, friendship. They can visit each other and even set up home somewhere else together. Seen in this way, mediation – the process of being in the middle – involves facilitation and conciliation, without pre-planned goals. It is a joint venture of working together to see what happens.

Mediation and peacemaking

Peacemaking is often perceived in essentially negative terms; namely as a type of conflict resolution. This view sees conflicts as fires, which need to be extinguished with a minimum of damage, and the conflict resolution specialists are firefighters. However, Scripture sees peacemaking in quite different terms as the continuous creation of harmonious relationships. Peacemaking is creative and continuous (never static) and proactive; it is not reactive firefighting, and it is far more profound than conflict resolution or peacekeeping. Peacemaking is what God has done through the blood of Jesus Christ shed on the cross (Colossians 1:20) and is what God continues to do as the gospel of Jesus Christ is extended throughout the world. Theologian Cornelius Plantinga writes:

> The webbing together of God, humans and all creation in justice, fulfilment and delight is what the Hebrew prophets call "shalom".

We call it "peace", but it means far more than mere peace of mind or the ceasefire between enemies. In the Bible "shalom" means universal flourishing, fullness and delight.[5]

In Scripture, peacemaking is the building of a harmonious network of relationships. They operate like four interlocking "circles": peace with God, peace with each other (what the Bible calls unity), peace with ourselves (peace of mind), and peace with the created natural order. There is an order of priority to these relationships. We are all seeking peace of mind, that elusive "satisfaction", but the witness of Scripture is that this is unavailable unless we are first at peace with God and then living at peace with each other and with the natural world. Scripture is essentially the story of peace. We are introduced in Genesis 1–2 to the creation of peace in each of these four dimensions (with God, with each other, with ourselves, and with creation). Peace was lost through the Fall (Genesis 3), and the rest of the story of the Bible from Genesis to Revelation is about the restoration of peace in each of these relationships through Jesus. As the apostle Peter declared, "You know the message God sent… announcing the good news of peace through Jesus Christ, who is Lord of all" (Acts 10:36; NIV).

So how does mediation fit into the wider range of peacemaking? There are, very broadly, two **inappropriate** responses to conflict, described by Ken Sande in his book *The Peacemaker: A Biblical Guide to Resolving Personal Conflict* (third edition, 2004). The first is *peace-faking*: denial followed by flight. This is the illusion that if I don't think about the issue, if I deny it and ignore it and concentrate on other things, it will just go away and things will be fine. They seldom are. The issue festers and unless dealt with usually leads to flight. To escape the problem you resign from your job, or move house, or file for divorce, or leave your congregation. This is where many Christians end up because of their misconception that all conflict is somehow sinful. However, most conflicts arise, at least initially, from difference (e.g. the different ways we see or think or respond or behave) rather than sin. What matters is how these differences, and the resulting disagreements, are dealt with. In contrast to the "flight" response there is the "fight" response. This is *peace-breaking*: aggression and assault, verbal or physical. Litigation between Christians can fall into this category (see 1 Corinthians 6:1–11).

There are equally two **appropriate** responses to conflict; what Ken Sande calls the *peacemaking* responses. The first type is "unassisted" peacemaking; you do it yourself. The second type requires help from other people, when it is impossible to achieve resolution on one's own. Whenever an issue is too significant to be overlooked then a "going" is required. In Matthew's Gospel we read the words of Jesus: "If your brother has something against you, leave your gift… first *go* and be reconciled to your brother" (Matthew 5:23–24); and "If your brother sins against you, *go* and show him his fault, just between the two of you" (Matthew 18:15). This seems to apply whether you are the offender or the offended. The principle is that the only thing you may not do is stay put! This "going" should lead to wise conversation, honesty, apology, repentance, forgiveness, and the like. If substantive rights are in issue, negotiation may be required too. But when for whatever reason there has been no initial "going", or if this "going" has not led to resolution, then the help of others is needed. This is where mediation comes in as part of the Christian commitment to peacemaking. If mediation fails then arbitration should be considered and a final stage of accountability and possibly corporate church discipline may be required.

The mediator's mindset

Mediation has consequences for the mediator. It is exhilarating when agreement against the odds breaks out. But there is a cost too. It can be very lonely, marooned in the middle in a sort of no-man's-land. I find myself increasingly stretched as I continue this work, particularly where I have my own opinions and judgments on the rightness or wrongness of the issues at stake, or the people involved in the mediation. Must I always be silent about what I think? Is neutrality allowed? Perhaps there is one answer to this question when mediating and another when in post-mediation mode? A dear friend recently wrote to me with the following (genuinely loving) criticism about an issue we were discussing:

> *Neutrality is a very comfortable position to take in the midst of controversy. No one enjoys conflict... So a middle position in which we don't have to take sides is very attractive. It claims to be neutral, and enables us to remain outside the controversy... I ask because one of our mutual friends, Stephen, said to me that in a recent meeting he asked you of your opinion in this area – to which he said your reply was, "In my position I don't have an opinion."*

To be honest I have not found it easy, or comfortable, to work through my responses to these questions (and the process is very much ongoing). I am also aware that I have much less familiarity in these areas than do many other mediators. Here, however, are five brief personal reflections.

First, I am not suggesting that mediation can solve fundamental moral or theological questions. However, the process whereby such questions are resolved – which inevitably involves discussion and debate – can always be facilitated and made more loving and kind.

Second, mediation is not carried out in a moral vacuum because in working with the parties all mediators have ethical obligations whenever issues of dishonesty and illegality arise.

Third, greater difficulty arises for me as a mediator where the dispute is about theological or moral issues on which I may have my own views which are different from those of some or all of those I am standing between. It is almost impossible properly to be a mediator and to be judgmental at the same time. My friend's critique links "neutrality" with "remaining outside the conflict". Personally I no longer use the (legal) terms "neutral" or "impartial" when describing my role. This is because they often give the wrong impression of distance from conflict or moral detachment, whereas by my own choice I am right in the middle of the conflict. Instead I use the term "multi-partial", and I aim to take both sides, with a hand on each shoulder, to relate to people with whom I may disagree.

Fourth, this is much easier said than done. It is not always easy to strike the right balance between who I am as a person and my role as a mediator. I find myself asking the question, "Where do I stand on these issues?" The answer, at least while I am mediating, is "In the middle... and suspended over a void". This can be profoundly uncomfortable particularly when, as often happens, I incline to the same answer after the mediation has finished. Having spent painful time in the middle, the old certainties sometimes seem less compelling. But, as my friend implied, are there not some issues that are too important to "duck" and on which it is necessary to choose one's side and on which it is cowardly (military term!) to remain publicly uncommitted? Is there not indeed a battle to be fought, a good fight to be waged, against wrongdoing and wrong thinking and evil, and in respect of which conscientious objection is unacceptable? Part of me increasingly questions these military metaphors that were so significant in my Christian upbringing. Another voice whispers that it is I who am the collaborator.

Fifth, my practice for many years was to pay lip service to the command to love those with whom I disagreed. I may now be at risk of the opposite danger, namely of seeking to avoid disagreeing with those whom I am learning to love.

Preparing ourselves for mediation

In their profound reflection on peacemaking, *Reconciling All Things: A Christian Vision for Justice, Peace and Healing* (2008), Emmanuel Katongole and Chris Rice suggest four fundamental disciplines for all those involved in this ministry:

STEP BACK

My tendency is to rush into disputes at breakneck speed believing that the sooner I get actively involved the better. One problem of behaving like this is that I arrive in the middle without any real perspective on those with whom I will be working or on the conflict in which they are stuck. Discipline is needed, right at the outset, to see clearly, deeply, and differently. Katongole and Rice encourage us first to step back, to pause, before plunging in; to pray to "receive God's imagination" for those with whom we will be involved. Scripture, as we ponder it, should inspire us about God's story, a move from old creation to new creation. It will challenge us – whatever peacemaking role we are seeking to fulfil – to examine ourselves, our motives, complicity, and responsibility. Before we help others, we are called to remove the plank from our own eye, so that we may "see clearly" (Matthew 5:3–5). This stepping back also helps us to think wisely about the conflict itself. What is it really about? What are the real issues? What might be achieved?

SLOW DOWN

Katongole and Rice remind us that Scripture speaks of the creation of peace and harmony out of a void, but that this gift of a peaceful creation took time. God's continuing recreation likewise still takes time. We need to cultivate the habits of peace. This involves slowing down. Our world by contrast is captivated by speed, and peacemaking becomes a form of engineering: pull the lever, press the button, and it is all visible progress. Reading God's story we see a different pattern, and one that suggests that we are not meant to be in a hurry. We need to apply this to our peacemaking initiatives. The two-hour meeting we are facilitating will almost certainly not bring to successful completion two years of acrimony between our friends. It may just be a single link in a long-term process.

LEARN TO LAMENT

As peacemakers, following Jesus, we will be called into places, and to be with people, of deep pain and brokenness. Lamenting, which is neither whingeing nor complaining, is a profound way of laying our hands on those we stand between. There is nothing we can do other than simply be there. There may be nothing to say. All we can do is listen, and lament, sometimes with tears. One of the profound questions asked of those participating in a recent facilitation between Christians (and which transformed the quality of the engagement) was this: "What has this dispute done to your soul?" Lament enables us to "unlearn speed": you cannot weep quickly; to "unlearn distance": you cannot remain at a safe distance; and, possibly most profoundly, to "unlearn innocence": I end up weeping in part for myself.

LOOK UP

By "looking up" Katongole and Rice encourage us to "practice resurrection". We cannot look upwards if we are running forwards; we fall over. But we can rest in the centre of chaos. There is a sequence in the film *Hotel Rwanda* (2004) where the militias have surrounded the hotel and the situation is desperate. The main characters drink champagne on the hotel rooftop. Katongole and Rice say this:

> ... *sabbath in a broken world is something like that – knowing in the midst of action when it is time to be still on the rooftop, even as the whole world is falling apart, spending time with the God we love. When the One we love whispers to us, "All will be well", it is more than wishful thinking. It is the fundamental truth of the universe. All will be well indeed... Sabbath is the time when we remember that we are in the hands of the God who rules the universe with love.*[6]

My friend Bill Marsh, who helped train me as a mediator, observed that as mediators we are, at one and the same time, both bearers of hope and agents of reality. "Looking up" is to remember that we speak a message of hope, for ourselves and for those whom we are with; that there is always, available every day, Jesus' promise that we may "receive the Holy Spirit".

The mediation process

There is no such thing as a typical mediation. The purpose of being in between individuals or groups of individuals who are at odds is to assist them to talk to each other; hopefully so that they can reach some agreements, and, in an ideal world, be reconciled, if not transformed, as a result of this process. Exactly how these objectives are most likely to be achieved will vary from case to case. The process is infinitely flexible. At one extreme (commercial mediations often involving large sums of money in dispute) there may be a more formal process involving lawyers, mini-submissions from expert witnesses, and then a negotiation about legal rights, litigation risk, and the like. Most commercial mediations involve one mediator only. A polarized church congregational dispute may involve months of preliminary work by facilitators, an initial scoping report, and then a series of meetings with groups of people. A neighbour dispute involves initial home visits by two mediators (usually one man and one woman) and then a short mediation. Victim offender mediation, also with two mediators, will involve a series of separate meetings with both victim and offender and their support groups before the two are brought together. In other situations the process could, however, just involve informal conversations between the mediator and the parties and may not even include a commitment to meet face to face in order to talk together.

Increasingly, business agreements include a provision that states that in the event of a dispute both sides will mediate. But in most situations there is no such underlying agreement, so someone, possibly one of the parties or perhaps more often a friend or family member, needs to design an intervention. Here are some questions to ask:

- What is the dispute really about? What may be going on below the surface?

- Who is able to mediate it? Who would be trusted? Who has the necessary skills? Should there be one or two mediators?

- Who are the key participants? Who needs to buy in to the mediation process? Whose agreement will be needed to bring the dispute to an end or to implement a workable solution on the ground?

- Does a written mediation agreement need to be made? If the dispute is about legal rights then the answer is yes. If not, then an informal summary from the mediator of the agreed process and ground rules sent to each participant is usually sufficient.

- Will the service be voluntary or will the mediator be paid?

- Who should attend the mediation on behalf of each party? What support might that person require from a family member or trusted friend or church pastor? Will that supporter buy in to the mediation process and work with, rather than against, the mediator?

- Where will the mediation take place? A church hall, a home, or somewhere more formal? Whatever the venue, it is important to ensure that each party has private space in which confidential discussions with the mediator can take place if needed.

- Is a pre-mediation statement beneficial? Sometimes each party exchanges a brief written statement with the other, laying out what they regard as the key issues, their objectives at the mediation, and what we call "grace" – namely, what they might be able to offer in order to try to bring about some form of resolution. Such statements are never easy, can be very challenging, and sometimes are inappropriate.

What is written or said, of course, is not always what it is all really about. But sometimes reading and pondering what the other has honestly written helps the healing process before the mediation itself begins.

Ken Sande, in *The Peacemaker*, uses the acronym GOSPEL to describe the six stages of the mediation: Ground rules and introduction, Opening statements, Storytelling, Problem identification and clarification, Exploring possible solutions, Leading to agreement. Ground rules will include respect, no interruptions, attempting to listen, and avoidance of abusive language or aggressive behaviour. The parties are encouraged to express their feelings and needs, doing their best to build compassionate communication and to avoid judgmental attitudes. Sometimes they may require guidance in how best to say things, for example with Nonviolent Communication methodology.[7] The mediation provides a safe space for conversation and real listening, and the sharing of stories at length. When participants ask how long to speak for, the best answer often is "until you feel that you've been heard".

The mediation may follow any of a wide number of courses. Sometimes the parties stay together for the entire process. Usually, at some stage, it is wise to take a break and for the mediators to have a private meeting, a caucus, with each individual group. At some stage "brainstorming" sessions often take place with each of those involved being invited to throw out possible solutions and to consider their respective advantages and disadvantages. The mediators seek to build rapport, to help each individual engage more effectively with those on the other side, to help them look for common interests and needs rather than wants, and to retain, as wisely as possible, "the hand on each shoulder".

Measuring success

Lawyers, as I have suggested, are preoccupied (rightly) with outcomes; mediators with the process in itself. As I pedal homewards to Wandsworth at one in the morning after a bruising mediation which has ended in acrimony, I remind myself that the conversations that have taken place and the relationships that I have built over the day with each side may themselves be a deep good. Sometimes, particularly for those individuals who feel disempowered and worthless, the mere fact that someone chooses to sit and listen, and to engage with their stories, is life changing. But it is not just about a laying of hands on different shoulders – powerful though this is. It is about what happens as a result of this.

Mediation, we have seen, is an intervention for the purpose of reaching some sort of agreement; an agreement between those who, until then, agreed about little if anything. If a successful mediation is the one that leads to "agreement", what does this look like? Is it a failure if the parties do not leave reconciled or transformed? I find it helpful to use an image of concentric circles (developed from Ken Cloke) to describe what "success" in an intervention might look like, with each outlying circle adding to, but incorporating, what has been achieved by the one inside. Moving from the inner to the outer, the smaller to the larger, they might be described as follows.

(a) *The process itself, or rather participation in it*: This is the innermost circle. The very fact that people have been prepared to travel somewhere, to meet with each other, to speak together and listen, is itself a success. Even if nothing else happens they usually leave with a sense of personal closure to some degree. Sometimes, it is true, their meeting merely confirms the worst that they thought about the other. But this is rare. Usually the meeting "humanizes" someone who until then had been a type of enemy. The American poet Henry Wadsworth Longfellow observed: "If we could read the secret history of our enemies, we should find in each man's life sorrow and suffering enough to disarm all hostility."[8] This is where conversation comes in. Lord Sacks, former

Chief Rabbi, wrote in his book *The Dignity of Difference*: "The greatest single antidote to violence is conversation."[9] At this inner and possibly most profound circle, success means no more than a softening of hearts. Sometimes hearts have become hardened through pain, anger, abuse, and aggression. But more often they have become numb to feeling, desensitized and deadened through conflict and theological jousting. The softening of hearts is a major achievement; any "agreement" beyond this is a bonus.

(b) *Ceasefire:* They decide to stop fighting. This ceasefire may be temporary or permanent. Many neighbour disputes are resolved through mediation by an agreement no longer to thump the ceiling at three in the morning in answer to noise upstairs or to insult each other when they meet in the lift. This also is no mean achievement.

(c) *Resolution of the defining issue:* The particular dispute is resolved between the parties. By "particular", I mean the one which manifests, the one which the parties themselves would identify, at least to an outsider, as the problem. Thus, the neighbours who have agreed a ceasefire now agree what to do in future when the same problem arises again. In the context of a legal dispute, resolution of the defining issue means the settlement of the litigation.

(d) *Resolution of the underlying issue:* Frequently there is more to the dispute than meets the eye and more to the dispute than the parties may express. Disputes within families or between individuals who have worked together for a long time often have this in common. It is the defining issue that brings them to the table but it is the safety of the process in which they are involved that enables them to disclose – sometimes even to discover – what it is that lies below the surface. Engagement of this nature frequently leads to a wider series of concentric circles.

(e) *Restitution:* This includes reparation, repentance, and apology. Apologies, in particular, can be enormously powerful. True apologies are often linked with a making good in some way – as illustrated in

215

the story of Zacchaeus in Luke 19. It is critical, however, to avoid what are known as "politicians' apologies". The first three words "I am sorry" sound great. But if the following words are "if" or "but" much of the power is lost and indeed the underlying offence may be repeated. Equally an apology that begins with the words "it may be that..." will rarely be of great impact.

(f) *Forgiveness:* This circle is a decision to forgive the wrongdoing, or a form of verbal blessing on the wrongdoer. Nelson Mandela is often quoted as stating: "Resentment is like drinking poison and then hoping it will kill your enemies."

(g) *Reconciliation:* The parties are restored to the relationship they enjoyed before the conflict arose. But because the process is costly, difficult, and painful, the emotion associated with reconciliation is frequently gratitude and empowerment. The parties have been on a journey and have, against the odds, triumphed.

(h) *Transformation:* Those who were distanced have reconciled. They were divided but are now united. In a truly transformative way, the whole is now greater than the sum of its parts. Conflict, when resolved by power or by a rights-focused approach (where a third party, a judge or arbitrator or other authority figure, produces or imposes a solution) *disempowers* those involved. Conflicts resolved by the immediate parties themselves, and by their journey together, *empower* them. They end up feeling better about themselves and about each other than they did at the outset.

Conclusion

The Irish poet W.B. Yeats wrote in 1919:

> *Things fall apart; the centre cannot hold*
> *Mere anarchy is loosed upon the world*

The blood-dimmed tide is loosed, and everywhere
The ceremony of innocence is drowned
The best lack all conviction, while the worst
Are full of passionate intensity.[10]

What may have been true in the aftermath of the First World War is even more applicable today. The risk of social fragmentation is immense. It is as if, at all levels of society, individuals, families, and groups of people who find themselves locked in conflict discover that they do not know what to say to each other, or how to say it, and so they say nothing. And when they say nothing, they turn their backs on each other and tend to move apart from each other. They polarize increasingly, leading lives of noisy desperation.

As the church seeks to discern the shape of God's mission in which we share today, it needs to recognize that the question "How do we live at peace?" is becoming one of the most profound cries of our age. Peacemaking at all levels is increasingly a matter of survival. The mediation phenomenon we are witnessing in the United Kingdom is a bit like the emergence of a "social antibody".[11] Just as in a human body antibodies develop to fight disease, so too societies threatened with polarization and fragmentation throw up groups of people whose role is to deal with this malaise.

This secular and sociological desperation for peace in a world looking for spiritual resources to face these challenges offers extraordinary opportunities for those whose belief system is based upon relational peace. The gospel with which we are entrusted points people to Jesus as the one mediator who brings us peace with God, and it also calls us as his followers to be peacemakers. As the body of Christ we need, in the face of our own conflicts and disagreements, to practise what we preach by working for peace among ourselves. That will in turn enable us to be seen and heard as bringers of good news as we enter into the mess of the world and stand in between those in conflict, seeking to transform it and them in the name of Jesus.

***

Questions

1. Have you ever acted as a mediator between people in conflict? Or have you had someone mediate a conflict in which you were involved? How did your experience compare to that described in this chapter?

2. Have you witnessed or been guilty of peace-faking (denial followed by flight) or peace-breaking? How can we engage instead in peacemaking?

3. When issues of serious error or sin are involved in a dispute, can a Christian mediator remain neutral in order to help all involved make peace?

4. Taking the four disciplines of peacemaking outlined here (step back, slow down, learn to lament, look up), what do you particularly need to cultivate and develop?

5. Given the world's need, what needs to change in the church for peacemaking to become part of our mission and message of good news?

Notes

1 DISAGREEING WITH GRACE

1. www.ergofabulous.org/luther.

2. Quoted in Andrew Atherstone, *Archbishop Justin Welby: Risk-taker and Reconciler* (London, 2014), p. 210.

3. John Stott, *"But I Say To You...": Christ the Controversialist* (new edition, Nottingham, 2013), p. 21.

4. Stott, *But I Say To You*, pp. 19–20.

5. Letter, 29 June 1750, in *The Works of the Reverend George Whitefield* (6 vols, London, 1771–72), vol. 2, p. 362.

6. John Wesley, *A Sermon on the Death of the Rev. Mr George Whitefield* (London, 1770), p. 23.

7. Baptist Tract Society, *The Primitive Church Magazine* (August 1851), p. 259.

8. Stott, *But I Say To You*, p. 19.

9. We are grateful to Bishop Keith Sinclair for these insights.

10. Paul Chang-Ha Lim, *In Pursuit of Purity, Unity, and Liberty: Richard Baxter's Puritan Ecclesiology in its Seventeenth-Century Context* (Leiden, 2004).

11. Mark D. Thompson, *A Clear and Present Word: The Clarity of Scripture* (Nottingham, 2006).

12. Articles 3 and 40 of the Forty-Two Articles (1553); see Gerald Bray (ed.), *Documents of the English Reformation* (Cambridge, 1994), pp. 286, 309.

13. Decree on Ecumenism, *Unitatis Redintegratio*, para. 11.

14. J.C. Ryle, "Best Means of Promoting Internal Unity in the Church", in *Nineteenth Annual Meeting of the Church Congress, Held at Swansea* (London, 1880), p. 384.

15. Quoted in Atherstone, *Archbishop Justin Welby*, p. 226.

16. Justin Welby, "Reconciliation in Nigeria", in R. John Elford (ed.), *Just Reconciliation: The Practice and Morality of Making Peace* (Bern, 2011), p. 66.

17. Quoted in Atherstone, *Archbishop Justin Welby*, pp. 131–32.

18. *General Synod: Report of Proceedings*, vol. 45 (July 2014), p. 311.

19. "Church of England to Have Women Bishops" (press release), 14 July 2014, www.churchofengland.org.

20. "Archbishop Addresses National Parliamentary Prayer Breakfast", 17 June 2014, www.archbishopofcanterbury.org.

21. Justin Welby, "Presidential Address", in *General Synod: Report of Proceedings*, vol. 45 (February 2014), p. 159.

22. "Statement from the College of Bishops", 27 January 2014, www.churchofengland.org.

23. *Shared Conversations on Sexuality, Scripture and Mission*, GS Misc 1083 (June 2014).

24. *Grace and Disagreement: Shared Conversations on Scripture, Mission, and Human Sexuality*, vol. 1: *Thinking Through the Process* (London, 2014), p. 33.

25. For a fuller defence of this view, see Martin Davie, "Why Disagreement is Not Good" (July 2014), www.mbarrattdavie. wordpress.com.

26. Ryle, "Best Means of Promoting Internal Unity", pp. 385–88.

27. Diocese of Oxford, *ad clerum*, October 2014.

2 RECONCILIATION IN THE NEW TESTAMENT

1. I am not suggesting that the origins of a word determine its meaning (the so-called "genetic fallacy"), but highlighting the way in which the origin of these words affects their meaning and use. On the genetic fallacy, see James Barr, *The Semantics of Biblical Language* (new edition, London, 2012) and Don Carson, *Exegetical Fallacies* (Grand Rapids, MI, 1996).

2. Ben Witherington, *The Acts of the Apostles* (Grand Rapids, MI, 2001), p. 269.

3. Anthony Thiselton, *The First Epistle to the Corinthians* (Grand Rapids, MI, 2013), pp. 519–525.

4. S.E. Porter, "Peace, Reconciliation" in Gerald F. Hawthorne, Ralph P. Martin, and Daniel G. Reid (eds), *Dictionary of Paul and His Letters* (Leicester, 1994), p. 696.

5. Porter, "Peace, Reconciliation".

6. It might be objected that the Jews, as God's chosen people, were hardly "hostile" to God. And yet, in line with his argument in Romans

2, Paul describes Jews ("we") as "children of wrath" as much as Gentiles (Ephesians 2:3).

7. R.P. Martin, "Center of Paul's Theology", in Hawthorne, Martin and Reid, *Dictionary of Paul and His Letters*, pp. 93–94. For a fuller defence of this, see R.P. Martin, *Reconciliation: A Study of Paul's Theology* (Grand Rapids, MI, 1989).

8. N.T. Wright, *Paul and the Faithfulness of God* (London, 2013), p. 12.

9. Wright, *Paul and the Faithfulness of God*, p. 16.

10. Wright, *Paul and the Faithfulness of God*, p. 30.

11. Michael Gorman, *Peace in Paul and Luke* (Cambridge, 2015), p. 8.

12. Alan Spence, *The Promise of Peace: A Unified Theory of Atonement* (London, 2006), p. 17.

13. Joel B. Green, *The Gospel of Luke* (Grand Rapids, MI, 1997), p. 291.

14. Perhaps the best exposition of the contrasts between John 3 and John 4 can be found in Mark Stibbe, *John* (Sheffield, 1993), pp. 62–64.

15. Gorman, *Peace in Paul and Luke*, pp. 8–9.

16. R.T. France, *The Gospel of Matthew* (Grand Rapids, MI, 2007), p. 408.

17. Green, *The Gospel of Luke*, pp. 579, 586.

18. Richard Bauckham, "James and the Gentiles", in Ben Witherington (ed.), *History, Literature, and Society in the Book of Acts* (Cambridge, 2007), pp. 172–73.

3   DIVISION AND DISCIPLINE IN THE NEW TESTAMENT CHURCH

1. This chapter is largely dependent on my Grove booklet, *When Should We Divide? Schism and Discipline in the New Testament* (Cambridge, 2004).

2. The Greek word for "division" in Luke 12:51 is *diamerismos*, a noun derived from a verb meaning "to divide up into parts", i.e. the opposite of unity.

3. These verses were never meant to be taken literally, but reflect by hyperbole the seriousness of temptations to sin.

4   PASTORAL THEOLOGY FOR PERPLEXING TOPICS

1. Ben Witherington, *The New Testament Story* (Grand Rapids, MI, 2004), p. 54.

5 GOOD DISAGREEMENT AND THE REFORMATION

1. Ernst Cassirer, Paul Oskar Kristeller, and John Herman Randall (eds), *The Renaissance Philosophy of Man* (Chicago, 1948), pp. 60, 85, 125–26.

2. Marjorie O'Rourke Boyle, *Erasmus on Language and Method in Theology* (Toronto, 1977), p. 73.

3. Henry Walter, *Doctrinal Treatises and Introductions to Different Portions of the Holy Scriptures by William Tyndale* (Cambridge, 1848), pp. liii–liv.

4. Walter, *Doctrinal Treatises*, p. lv.

5. *The Whole Workes of W. Tyndall, Iohn Frith and Doct. Barnes* (1573), Section Two (Works of Frith), pp. 126, 145.

6. Walter, *Doctrinal Treatises*, p. 384.

7. Walter, *Doctrinal Treatises,* pp. 374, 381.

8. Walter, *Doctrinal Treatises*, pp. 381, 385.

9. Diarmaid MacCulloch, *Thomas Cranmer: A Life* (New Haven, CT, 1996), pp. 525–29.

6 ECUMENICAL (DIS)AGREEMENTS

1. E.J. Poole-Connor, *Evangelical Unity* (London, 1941), pp. 13, 190.

2. David B. Barrett, George T. Kurian, and Todd M. Johnson (eds), *World Christian Encyclopedia: A Comparative Survey of Churches and Religions in the Modern World* (second edition, Oxford, 2001), vol. 1, pp. 16–18.

3. Kathryn Spink, *A Universal Heart: The Life and Vision of Brother Roger of Taizé* (third edition, London, 2015).

4. George Carey, *The Church in the Market Place* (new edition, Eastbourne, 1995), pp. 13–16. See further, Andrew Atherstone, "Archbishop Carey's Ecumenical Vision", *Theology* vol. 106 (September 2003), pp. 342–52.

5. George Carey, *Canterbury Letters to the Future* (Eastbourne, 1998), p. 188.

6. George Carey, *The Meeting of the Waters: A Balanced Contribution to the Ecumenical Debate* (London, 1985), pp. 25, 134, 136.

7. Mark Noll, *American Evangelical Christianity: An Introduction* (Oxford, 2001), p. 50.

8. *Just As I Am: The Autobiography of Billy Graham* (New York, 1997), p. 303.

9. David Frost, *Billy Graham in Conversation* (Oxford, 1998), p. 68. For

critique of Graham's approach, see Iain Murray, *Evangelicalism Divided* (Edinburgh, 2000), chapters 2–3.

10. *The Nottingham Statement* (London, 1977), p. 44.

11. David L. Edwards and John Stott, *Essentials: A Liberal-Evangelical Dialogue* (London, 1988).

12. Bernard Barlow, *"A Brother Knocking at the Door": The Malines Conversations 1921–1925* (Norwich, 1996).

13. Charles Colson and Richard John Neuhaus (eds), *Evangelicals and Catholics Together: Toward a Common Mission* (London, 1996), p. ix.

14. See further, Walter Kasper, *Harvesting the Fruits: Basic Aspects of Christian Faith in Ecumenical Dialogue* (London, 2009).

15. Francis Clark, *Eucharistic Sacrifice and the Reformation* (London, 1960), p. 522.

16. J.I. Packer, "The Good Confession", in J.I. Packer (ed.), *Guidelines* (London, 1967), pp. 15–16.

17. P.E. Hughes, "The Credibility of the Church", in Packer, *Guidelines*, pp. 170–71.

18. Donald Macleod, "The Basis of Christian Unity", *Evangel* vol. 3 (Autumn 1985), p. 6.

19. G.K.A. Bell (ed.), *Documents on Christian Unity 1920–4* (Oxford, 1924), pp. 2–3.

20. *The New Delhi Report: The Third Assembly of the World Council of Churches 1961* (London, 1962), p. 116.

21. Colin Buchanan, Graham Leonard, Eric Mascall, and J.I. Packer, *Growing into Union: Proposals for Forming a United Church in England* (London, 1970), pp. 97, 131, 158.

22. For an overview, see especially Ruth Rouse and Stephen Neill (eds), *A History of the Ecumenical Movement 1517–1948* (third edition, Geneva, 1986); Harold Fey (ed.), *The Ecumenical Advance: A History of the Ecumenical Movement 1948–1968* (second edition, Geneva, 1986).

23. Mark D. Chapman, *The Fantasy of Reunion: Anglicans, Catholics, and Ecumenism, 1833–1882* (Oxford, 2014).

24. Andrew Atherstone, "The Keele Congress of 1967: A Paradigm Shift in Anglican Evangelical Attitudes", *Journal of Anglican Studies* vol. 9 (November 2011), pp. 175–97.

25. Leuenberg Agreement (1973), www.leuenberg.net.

26. *The Church of Jesus Christ* (Frankfurt am Main, 1995), p. 121.

27. Quoted in Hanfried Krüger, "The Life and Activities of the World Council of Churches", in Fey, *Ecumenical Advance*, pp. 35–36.

28. John Stott, *Christ the Controversialist* (London, 1970), pp. 21–22.

29. David Middleton, *A Time to Unite* (London, 1968), p. 59.

30. Macleod, "The Basis of Christian Unity", p. 6.

31. Quoted in Andrew Atherstone, *Archbishop Justin Welby: Risk-taker and Reconciler* (London, 2014), p. 131.

32. *Ut Unum Sint*, para. 20.

33. "Common Declaration by Pope John Paul II and the Archbishop of Canterbury", *One in Christ* vol. 33 (1997), p. 78.

34. George Carey, *Sharing a Vision* (London, 1993), p. 147.

35. George Carey, "The Nature of Ecumenical Vision: Sermon in Luxembourg Cathedral", *One in Christ* vol. 34 (1998), pp. 193–94.

36. George Carey, *I Believe* (London, 1991), pp. 27, 118.

37. Quoted in Atherstone, *Archbishop Justin Welby*, p. 131.

7 GOOD DISAGREEMENT BETWEEN RELIGIONS

1. Adam B. Seligman, "Pedagogic Principles for the Production of Knowledge in Deeply Plural Societies", in Donald W. Harward (ed.), *Civic Values, Civic Practices* (Washington, DC, 2013), p. 58. See also his *Living with Difference: How to Build Community in a Divided World*, with Rahel R. Wasserfall and David W. Montgomery (Oakland, CA, 2016). For CEDAR (Communities Engaging with Difference and Religion), see www.cedarnetwork.org.

2. Marshall Rosenberg, *Nonviolent Communication: A Language of Life* (Encinitas, CA, 2003).

3. Brian K. Pennington, *Was Hinduism Invented? Britons, Indians, and the Colonial Construction of Religion* (Oxford, 2005); Geoffrey A. Oddie, *Imagined Hinduism: British Protestant Missionary Constructions of Hinduism, 1793–1900* (London, 2006).

4. "Pluralism – public and religious", in Rowan Williams, *Faith in the Public Square* (London, 2012), chapter 10.

5. Danielle S. Allen, *Talking to Strangers: Anxieties of Citizenship since Brown v. Board of Education* (Chicago, 2004), p. 118.

6. Walter Brueggemann, *Genesis* (Atlanta, 1982), p. 267.

8 FROM CASTLES TO CONVERSATIONS

1. Egalitarians and complementarians agree that all people are created equal in dignity, value, essence, and human nature (ontological equality). Complementarians believe that men and women are distinct in role (Genesis 2; 1 Corinthians 11:2–15; 1 Timothy 2:11–15) and that although the Fall distorted this role-relationship (e.g. some women having a desire to usurp the authority of men and some men leading in an unloving and domineering way) redemption through Christ means restored role differentiation in the home and church. Egalitarians stress equal responsibility to rule over creation (Genesis 1:26–28) and emphasize mutuality rather than roles in male–female relationship pre-Fall. They see the Fall introducing hierarchy into the relationship between men and women (Genesis 3:16), which is overcome in Christ where redemption restores equality (Galatians 3:28).

2. "On the Gender Agenda" (2 February 2011), www.ellidhcook. wordpress.com.

3. Review by Colin Randall at Fellowship of Word and Spirit, www.fows. org.

4. Review by Jenny Baker (1 January 2011) at Sophia Network, www.blog. sophianetwork.org.uk.

5. Lis Goddard and Clare Hendry, *The Gender Agenda: Discovering God's Plan for Church Leadership* (Nottingham, 2010), foreword.

6. For the papers and statements from the AWESOME–Reform conversations, see www.awesome.org.uk.

7. See further, "An Affirmation of Evangelical Unity over the Theology of Women and Men", bringing together people who disagree on the subject, www.affirmingevangelicalunity.com.

9 MINISTRY IN SAMARIA

1. Matthew Levering, *Participatory Biblical Exegesis: A Theology of Biblical Interpretation* (Notre Dame, IN, 2008), p. 148.

2. John Hayes and Sara Mandell, *The Jewish People in Classical Antiquity* (Louisville, KY, 1998).

3. This is a major theme of Jesus' "short-term" peace mission in and around Samaria in Luke 9:51 – 19:44, which carries over into the mission of the apostles in Acts; see Paul Borgman, *The Way According to Luke* (Grand Rapids, MI, 2006), pp. 77–96.

4. Robert Alter, *The Art of Biblical Narrative* (London, 1981), pp. 52–57.

5. See further Ben Witherington, *John's Wisdom: A Commentary on the Fourth Gospel* (Cambridge, 1995), pp. 115–25; Adeline Fehribach, *The Women in the Life of the Bridegroom* (Collegeville, MN, 1998), pp. 45–81; and especially Jocelyn McWhirter, *The Bridegroom Messiah and the People of God: Marriage in the Fourth Gospel* (Cambridge, 2006).

6. Steven McMichael, "Francis and the Encounter with the Sultan (1219)", in Michael J.P. Robson (ed.), *Cambridge Companion to Francis of Assisi* (Cambridge, 2012), pp. 127–42.

7. Ignacio Larranaga, *Brother Francis of Assisi* (Quebec, 1989), p. 201.

8. The conference talks were published as Kelly James Clark (ed.), *Abraham's Children: Liberty and Tolerance in an Age of Religious Conflict* (New Haven, CT, 2012).

9. See, for example, Miroslav Volf's conversation with Sheik Habib Ali al-Jifri, in *Allah: A Christian Response* (New York, 2011), pp. 127–48.

10. Joel C. Elowsky (ed.), *Ancient Christian Commentary of Scripture: New Testament*, vol. IVa: John 1–10 (Downers Grove, IL, 2006), p. 147.

11. Patrick Reardon, *Christ in His Saints* (Ben Lomond, CA, 2004), p. 27.

12. Elizabeth Stopp, *A Man to Heal Differences: Essays and Talks on St Francis de Sales* (Philadelphia, 1997), p. 196.

13. Stopp, *A Man to Heal Differences*, p. 195.

14. The whole intriguing episode merits reflection as a seminal instance of peacemaking between Christians; see André Ravier, *Francis de Sales: Sage and Saint* (San Francisco, 1988), pp. 79–95.

15. A year later I learned that Shannon's father had been a poetry professor, and, as he said to me, "I trust poetry more than prose. For something to be true it must be true in the heart not just the head." It turned out to be the perfect gift, both "well and water" combined.

16. At Truro Church, we have not yet entered this "third moment" of peacemaking with any of our former adversaries. More work remains to be done on the road of peace.

17. Augustine, *Sermo Suppositus*, 120.

18. Paul Chilcote, *She Offered Them Christ: The Legacy of Women Preachers in Early Methodism* (Nashville, TN, 1993).

19. *The Works of John Wesley* (Nashville, TN and Oxford, 1984–), vol. 26, p. 206.

20. *The Works of John Wesley*, vol. 2, p. 510.

21. For the definitive account of the movement's effect in North America, which explains and illustrates Truro's experience, see Grant Wacker's *Heaven Below: Early Pentecostals and American Culture* (Cambridge, MA, 2001).

10 MEDIATION AND THE CHURCH'S MISSION

1. Many others have wider experience in mediation, especially in the church. For further resources and training, see the work of Bridge Builders (www.bbministries.org.uk).

2. I have never worked as a criminal barrister and what I say about the Bar applies only to civil dispute resolution and not to the workings of the criminal courts, which are concerned with quite different criteria. Nor have I worked as a family (divorce) lawyer where significant mediation is now taking place.

3. There is absolutely no parallel intended with the movie of the same name!

4. Faidi & Anor v Elliot Corporation [2012] EWCA (England and Wales Court of Appeal) Civ 287

5. Cornelius Plantinga, *Not the Way It's Supposed To Be: A Breviary of Sin* (Grand Rapids, MI, 1995), p. 10.

6. Emmanuel Katongole and Chris Rice, *Reconciling All Things: A Christian Vision for Justice, Peace and Healing* (Downers Grove, IL, 2008), p. 45.

7. Marshall Rosenberg, *Nonviolent Communication: A Language of Life* (Encinitas, CA, 2003); Susan Scott, *Fierce Conversations: Achieving Success in Work and in Life, One Conversation at a Time* (London, 2002).

8. 'Driftwood", in *The Prose Works of Henry Wadsworth Longfellow* (London, 1874), p. 776.

9. Jonathan Sacks, *The Dignity of Difference: How to Avoid the Clash of Civilizations* (London, 2002), p. 2.

10. "The Second Coming", lines 3–8, in W.B. Yeats, *Michael Robartes and the Dancer* (Churchtown, Ireland, 1921).

11. Stephen Ruttle, "Mediation: A Social Antibody?", Roebuck Lecture 2013, *Arbitration* vol. 79 (August 2013), pp. 295–308.